The Village of Bom Jesus

The Village of Bom Jesus

Fiction by Lloyd E. Hill

Algonquin Books of Chapel Hill

1993

Published by Algonquin Books of Chapel Hill
Post Office Box 2225
Chapel Hill, North Carolina 27515-2225
a division of
Workman Publishing Company, Inc.
708 Broadway
New York, New York 10003

This is a work of fiction. While, as in all fiction, the
literary perceptions and insights are based on experience, all
names, characters, places, and incidents are either products of
the author's imagination or are used fictitiously. No reference
to any real person is intended or should be inferred.

Library of Congress Cataloging-in-Publication Data
Hill, Lloyd E., 1938–
The village of Bom Jesus / Lloyd E. Hill.
p.   cm.
ISBN 0-945575-88-2
1. Rain forests—Brazil—Fiction.   2. Villages—Brazil—Fiction.
3. Cats—Fiction.   I. Title.
ps3558.1396v54   1993
813'.54—dc20   92-36306 CIP

2   4   6   8   10   9   7   5   3   1

First Edition

With love, this book is dedicated to

Sonya Angela

Lloyd Joaquim

Mary Jane

Angela Nicole

Ashley Ann

Kimberly Nicole

Kevin Daniel

and

Jennifer Marie

Contents

The Village of Bom Jesus

The First We Hear of Bom Jesus

O Bom Jesus (The Good Jesus) was a calico cat most enigmatic. A vagary in a land that forbade vagaries. A cat who thought that he was a dog.

Along the muddy banks of the Juruá River a cat was seldom seen. Yet, early one rainy morning, somehow, from somewhere, the bedraggled mother of Bom Jesus found her way to the doorstep of one João Daví, a gnarled and weatherbeaten old fisherman who lived on the outskirts of the tiny hamlet of Guajará.

João Daví wasn't sure of his exact age; only that he had been born before the turn of the century. Also, that it had been, indeed, many years since his snow-white hair had been dark auburn in color. He did remember, to the hour, that day some eleven years earlier when his wife, Dona Maria, had died of some nameless fever here in the backwaters of that region called "the world's backside" by more sophisticated Brazilians. Almost to the day, he also knew when each of his eight children had left in search of new lives twenty miles upriver in the small city of Cruzeiro do Sul, and downriver in the steamy environs of the metropolis of Manaus, hundreds of miles away. His last remaining son had left one day in his canoe for Belém, a city near the mouth of the Amazon, thousands of river miles away. For many days he had rowed and drifted with the currents down the twisting Juruá to its confluence with the Solimões (the name Brazilians use for this stretch of the Amazon), where he sold his canoe and bought passage on the *Lauro Soudré,* one of the Dutch-built paddlewheelers that ply the rivers of Northern Brazil. João Daví doubted that he'd ever see him again.

Unaccustomed to a house without sound, without laughter, yelling, crying, and conversation, he began to accumulate all the strays who invariably found his house the most sympathetic in the neighborhood. Among his new family was a coati called Rabão; a parrot called Bobão; three dogs—one female and two males—called Cebolinha, Rato, and Peixe; and a squirrel he had never gotten around to naming.

In this small zoo, Bom Jesus's mother found acceptance, albeit after many beatings administered to Cebolinha, Rato, and Peixe by the old man. Bom Jesus's mother had one thing in common with Cebolinha. They were both fat with wiggly offspring.

At two o'clock one early morning, amid soft snores coming from João Daví's hammock and muted rustlings of tiny bats in the palm-frond roof, Cebolinha gave birth to her first litter. Six mouse-sized, hungry pups. As if jealous, Bom Jesus's mother had her first litter: five miniature, speckled kittens, mewing with surprise at being born.

At ten o'clock that same morning, the old man stuck his head out the window and called to his favorite neighbor, a raven-haired seven-year-old by the name of Maria Fatima de Souza. "Fatima. Come here. Come see what I found this morning."

"What is it, *seu* João?" she asked. "I have to fetch some medicine from *seu* Estevão."

"Come and see. It's a surprise."

Hearing this, Fatima hurried up the dangerously fragile old wooden steps and found herself confronted with a most wondrous sight. There, resting side by side, were Cebolinha and Bom Jesus's mother, and eleven squirming little imps, noisily suckling away.

"Oh, *seu* João. How beautiful. Look! Cebolinha has a kitten and your cat has two puppies. They're all mixed up."

The old man laughed. "Beautiful, yes. But, what am I to do with eleven new stomachs to feed? I now have the only menagerie in town. Probably the only one in a thousand kilometers."

"What's a menagerie?"

"It's a place where they keep all kinds of strange animals. I saw one in São Paulo once, years and years ago."

"You must let me keep them for you," Fatima declared.

"I would love to have you keep them for me, my sweet Fatima. But you know that your mother won't let you have animals in the house."

"Oh, *Mamãe* is mean. Why doesn't she like animals? They're so nice."

"Your mother isn't mean. She just likes to keep a clean house," the old man replied.

"Here's what we'll do," he said. "You pick one kitten, and we can train it to jump through the window into

· · · · ·
4

your room. That way you can play with it any time you like."

"Yes. You're so smart. Can I pick one now?"

"Go ahead. I'll go get your medicine for you while you watch over them. Pick the prettiest one."

As old João left for *seu* Estevão's house, Fatima turned to study her newfound treasures. Which one? Which one? she thought. Immediately, her large brown eyes alighted upon the speckled baby who had mistaken Cebolinha for its mother.

"You poor blind little thing," she said aloud. "Don't you know which one is your mother? I hope you have blue eyes."

Cautiously she reached out and lifted the warm, weak little body. At the same time, she patted Cebolinha, to allay her fears for her adopted child.

As the two mothers watched with some trepidation, Fatima studied her new pet, and delicately stroked its head while it nuzzled her fingers searching for the teat it had lost.

She found that it had a mostly white head with a black patch around its mouth, giving it the appearance of having a beard. Its body was splattered with all kinds of cat-colors. And, so what if its eyes weren't blue? But maybe they would be. Its mother's eyes were bright cornflowers.

· · · · ·
5

Without a clue as to whether or not it was a female or male (it grew into a very big, sometimes ferocious, sometimes exceedingly gentle and friendly tom cat), Fatima decided to call it "Baby Jesus," but feeling that this might be irreverent, irreverently renamed it "Good Jesus." "*Bom Jesus.*"

When the kittens were three weeks old, their mother disappeared—probably the victim of a hungry jaguar that had prowled the surrounding farms before being driven off by a pack of village dogs. Or probably she was the victim of this same pack of dogs. No one ever found out.

This was an unwelcome and sad quandary for old João Daví and Maria Fatima. Cebolinha was happily accustomed to feeding kittens and puppies alike. But eleven? They eventually solved this problem by stuffing Cebolinha with all kinds of meats—choice bits of beef, anteater, iguana, squirrel, and an occasional roasted piranha—and by making sure that each of the eleven got its turn. As they got older, João traded freshly caught catfish for freshly pulled cow's milk, and fed this to them. All survived and waxed healthy and round-bellied.

Four of the calico kittens grew into regular cats, imbued by nature with cat ways and manners. *O* Bom Jesus, no. Bom Jesus loved the earthy dog-smell of his foster mother, Cebolinha. *Cebolinha* (Little Onion) was aptly named. She delighted in wallowing with the neighbors' pigs, uprooting cow chips with her moist nose, and chasing every strange animal she encountered. These offensive-to-man odors she brought into the house were delightful-to-cat perfumes for Bom Jesus.

Bom Jesus found more pleasure chewing on, playing with, licking, and sleeping with his brother and sister pups than with his sibling kittens. Although when the pups tired of his rough play, he would switch over to the rested kittens, eventually making them weary enough to find a hiding place in which to lick their fur and take a lazy nap.

As the years went by, the kittens and puppies were dispersed to people near and far. Not Bom Jesus. Fatima and old João had found a beloved friend and helpful ally with whom to face the sometimes perilous life of this never-heard-of land.

Bom Jesus was a strange, favorite personage who found himself the subject of interest among the villagers whenever conversations lagged around the dinner table or at the schoolyard. No one could ever recall having seen a male calico cat. Especially was he talked about over a bottle of vermouth or *cachaça* at the corner *botequim*.

Debates about his usefulness as compared to his peskiness were generally decided in his favor. Among his bad traits were chasing chickens (after several bruising swats with brooms and sticks, he learned not to indulge himself in this merry pastime) and sneaking into folks' houses late at night, noisily investigating cupboards and bedrooms; often, he found flower beds nice places in which to roll around and dust himself.

Overshadowing and far outweighing these impish misdeeds was one decidedly helpful beneficence he bestowed upon the entire village. He kept at bay every poisonous snake that wandered in from the dank river bottoms nearby. Uncannily he seldom bothered the harmless ones, unless, of course, he was in an especially playful mood.

To Bom Jesus, an angry snake was a wonderful playmate. Like a happy mongoose, he became expert at dodging their deadly strikes. Usually he would jump high in the air and land completely turned around, facing the back of the snake before it could finish recoiling. Sometimes, as a change of pace, he would jump backwards, stopping almost, but not quite, within reach of the sharp fangs. Once, he was seen to calmly step to one side, almost as if he were imitating an adroit bullfighter, avoiding being bitten by the breadth of one of his fine whiskers.

After dispatching his erstwhile playfellows, Bom Jesus would drag them to the nearest house and deposit them on the front steps. He did this in repayment of the scraps of food and bowls of milk the friendly villagers gave him whenèver he appeared during mealtimes. He probably never found out that his gifts were surreptitiously buried in back yards or thrown into the river.

Bom Jesus's generosity with his dead snakes caused much commotion one night when he brought a particularly large and venomous fer-de-lance into the small, one-room house of the widow, Dona Pipira. Dona Pipira was, next to Fatima and João Daví, and Fatima's friend, Mariquinha, his favorite human. Besides providing him with bowls of milk and leftover bones, she usually placed a tasty meal of fish soup beneath the table, awaiting his nocturnal visits. This certain night, Dona Pipira was next door visiting her neighbors. Bom Jesus, departing from his usual custom of leaving the snake on her doorstep, thought that, since the fer-de-lance was such a fine specimen of inglorious snakehood, he would leave it on her table.

After much pulling and laborious dragging, Bom Jesus managed to accomplish his well-intentioned task. He had just sat down to rest and admire his handiwork when the widow chose this moment to return, candle in hand. When she saw the horrible present, she let out a screech that awakened half the village. As was her wont at times of extreme stress she fainted, falling among her pots and pans with such a crash that the other half of the village awoke. This startled Bom Jesus, who leaped towards the ceiling and, rebounding off the table, flew through the window, landing feet first, claws extended, on Dona Pipira's cow. This caused the cow to bellow so loudly that the jungle came alive with frightened animal sounds of all descriptions.

Almost an hour passed before everyone quieted down. After ascertaining what had happened, the neighbors went home one by one. Dona Pipira had revived, still weak from shock but improving, and Bom Jesus had snuck into Fatima's room and fallen asleep on her bed, dreaming of snakes, screams, and sundry witcheries.

The kind-hearted Dona Pipira forgave Bom Jesus, although, forever after, she steeled herself before entering her house after dark, expecting another of Bom Jesus's thoroughly disgusting dead friends.

This was only one of many such incidents in the life of the villagers' pet cat. Most of his troubles came from chasing small animals—not to kill them, but to find out whether or not they wanted to play. There was the time when he lost a toe to a voracious piranha while trying to catch a frog on the banks of a swampy, black-watered lake behind the village called, with funereal but understandable logic, *O Lago das Mortes* (The Lake of the Dead).

On another occasion he fell into this same evil-smelling, murky lake after fruitlessly chasing a butterfly along a rotted overhanging limb, which broke under his weight. This time he escaped the piranhas but, with the worst luck, received a painful shock from a hungry electric eel. He was shaky for almost a week afterwards.

Of such events, small legends are made, becoming more heroic or more foolish with the passing of the years.

Bom Jesus made friends with, or, alternately, whipped every dog in Guajará. He hung out with all the packs, chasing wild animals, roughhousing, and often napping and lolling about with his panting, larger comrades. He couldn't bark, but he had an eerie, frightening growl. Visitors to town, rugged frontiersmen all, and accustomed to yapping mongrels, were terrified to find a large, bescarred, bewhiskered cat charging them from afar, only letting them pass after sniffing their feet as if warning them that he would remember who they were if they happened to misbehave. Cats just don't do such things.

One poor nun who had come to help the villagers with novena in the absence of a priest, and who wasn't at all a frontiersman, was sent screaming down the dusty streets, yelling, "Mad cat! Mad cat!" When she had calmed down and had been told that it was only the Good Jesus who was chasing her, her first befuddled thought was, Dear God, these people need a priest immediately!

João Daví soon learned that Bom Jesus was a better hunting companion than his three dogs. He moved more silently than they did through heavy underbrush, and, without once failing, located all the game old João felled with his rusted muzzleloader. He did have one bad fault, however. Whenever the old man shot an animal, Bom Jesus would bring it back if it was small, or, if it was large, sit on top of it and mew until his master found him; but, if it was a bird, his cat's nature would overwhelm him and he usually brought back only a mouthful of feathers.

Soon all the huntsmen were borrowing Bom Jesus. Larders thereafter were seldom empty. His bad habit of eating birds was made to work to the hunter's advantage. They simply shot more than Bom Jesus's stomach could hold. This always made him eager to go hunting with anyone who came looking for him. Even Paulo Moraes, who made his living by trapping for animal hides, would borrow him for short trips into the jungle.

Few outsiders came this far up the Juruá. Most of those who stayed were Irish and German priests and nuns. One of these, Father O'Malley, visited Guajará once a month for Sunday Mass. He always delighted in taking Bom Jesus for long walks into the deep forest, as did old Estevão, who spent many hours collecting herbs and roots. When he had spare time, Father O'Malley joined *seu* Estevão and Bom Jesus on these collecting trips. Indeed, it was a strange sight to see: a tall, green-eyed priest, a crooked old man, and a calico cat squatting in a mossy glade inspecting a seemingly ordinary leaf, or a piece of shaggy bark.

A strange sight? Yes. But no stranger than many. You see, the swamps and high jungles of the Juruá are home to a multitude of strange things, and we have heard many tales from Guajará, the village of Bom Jesus.

A New Kind of Curandeiro

Arriving in Cruzeiro do Sul on the same airplane as the provisional prefect of the newly created prefecture of Guajará was a southerner from São Paulo. His name was Adão Braga Oliveira. Of a little more than average height, he had black hair, brown eyes, and a pale, easily sunburned complexion. Although not stockily built, he gave an impression of immense physical strength.

The long trip from the state capital, Manaus, takes

anywhere from one day to two weeks, depending on the length of stopovers. This trip was one of the more time-consuming ones—one week and five days. During these interminably boring days and nights, *seu* Jader, the temporary prefect, and Adão became close friends, finding in each other kindred intellects, interested in all matters, whether mundane, worldly, or esoteric.

The prefect, taking a sincere liking to the younger man—twenty-six years as compared to his forty-one—convinced him to change his plan of building a farm and small rubber plantation in Acre, to one of buying or homesteading land across the border, in his new prefecture, in the state of Amazonas. By the time they had taken the hour-and-a-half boat ride downriver from Cruzeiro do Sul to Guajará, the prefect had insisted on hiring Adão as a part-time secretary, so that he could live at state expense in the new two-room government building (a converted house that had been freshly white-washed and reroofed with tile instead of palm fronds), and could eat at state expense next door, at *seu* Bonifacio's and Dona Santa's house.

Adão, an easy-going, mild-tempered man who was never grasping or inclined to seek advantage at another's expense, nevertheless accepted opportunities whenever they appeared. Here was a homesteader's dream realized. A job that paid him room and board and left him with all the time he needed to build his farm. Of course he accepted. And, there being no difference in the quality of land in this part of southern Amazonas and of that in Acre, he decided to make his home nearby.

Instead of homesteading free land deep in the jungle, he bought a square mile of river-fronted forest, halfway between Guajará and the settlement of Floresta. He paid the prefecture a nominal fee for the land with part of a small inheritance his grandfather had left him. It was bottom land, the best suited for the rubber trees he intended to plant.

He got along well with the inhabitants of Guajará. They were friendly by nature, and so was he. He did have some minor problems with the language. His southern-accented Portuguese was much harsher and much more correct than the softer local drawl of these *Amazonenses*. Also, some of their words were completely different from his own. But these difficulties were quickly overcome.

There was one small inconsistency that he could never surmount, no matter how hard he tried. He could rarely get anyone to call him Adão. It was always "*seu* Adão," or "*O Senhor*," or "*Senhor* Oliveira." Others might enjoy the respect that was intended, but not Adão.

He had a need, a deeply buried one, to be accepted by everyone, no matter how unimportant they were in his life. Respect is not always complete acceptance.

He understood some of the reasons for this respect. The main ones were his employment at the prefecture and his obvious education. One reason escaped him at first. This was the aura of mystery that obscured his reason for coming to Guajará. Why here? Why not the more accessible state of Pará, or Minas Gerais or Mato Grosso? Guajará was at the end of the world. Except for tiny river settlements and the small city of Cruzeiro do Sul, over in Acre, no one lived there. One could leave the banks of the Juruá and trek through the forest in any direction and, within a matter of minutes, step upon never-trodden ground. There was nothing but jungle for mile after endless mile. A few refugees came from neighboring Peru for political or criminal reasons. Was this why Adão had come? Had he committed a serious crime? Were his politics shady? Had he had a heart-breaking love affair? He never satisfactorily explained the reasons. His answer, "Because there are many opportunities here," was too vague. Still, notwithstanding this minor puzzle, he was well liked. This was what was important.

Soon after buying his land, Adão settled into a routine of working from early morning until almost dark, clearing it of trees and brush. At night he typed occasional letters for the prefect, and enjoyed Sundays off by fishing or hunting in the daytime and by drinking moderately—two or three times immoderately—with the men down at the *botequim*, which was, in this case, a combination general store and saloon. Sometimes he would go to the dances that were held at the two-room wooden schoolhouse, flirting with the village girls. All of them found him agreeable, though somewhat aloof.

It took him four months to clear the parts of his land that were in the flood plain of the river and some of the higher ground. He did this by chopping away the brush and the smaller trees with a machete, then returning to the larger trees with an axe.

Four months was record time, even for the hardworking locals, but Adão was exceptionally strong, and willing to overlook the discomforts that the work entailed. Besides the aching, blistering labor of swinging a heavy axe all day, there are always miscellaneous unpleasantries. Banging an axe against any jungle tree always jars loose something from above, especially in the bottom lands. You can expect a shower of biting ants, stinging bees or wasps, a frightened spider, a rare scorpion or an even rarer snake. Not everyone is suited to this kind of work.

Taking a bath after work was another minor problem.

At home in São Paulo, Adão had been used to bathing in a modern shower, with its usual tile walls and floor and curtain for privacy. Here, the natives divided among the men and women a clear, idyllic jungle brook with fast-running water. The only problem: it was full of piranhas. It took him a while to learn that the piranhas were generally harmless except in backwaters and stagnant lakes, or if someone had a fresh wound that bled too freely, which could turn the little fish from docile, finny creatures into insatiable biting machines.

At first, Adão would squat beside the bank and dump water, dipped from the brook with half of a coconut shell, over his head and body. But, feeling cowardly after seeing everyone else diving and swimming and in general having a good time among those dreaded meat-eaters, he shakily jumped in with them, expecting to be reduced to a skeleton within seconds. It was not to be. After watching two piranhas and a tiny catfish swim up and inspect his naked body, and then swim inscrutably away, Adão nonchalantly (outwardly, not inwardly) had a fine time lazing around, trading gossip, splashing water, and being splashed in turn by his new friends.

▼

It was shortly after he had completed the first phase of clearing his land that something happened that reversed forever the direction his life was taking.

It was about four weeks before the end of the dry season. He had planned to spend his days hunting and fishing until just before the rains were due to start. Then, he was going to set fire to all the brush and trees he had felled. This would cleanse the land of all but the largest logs.

Eventually, he would be able to set fire to his land, but his plans for hunting and fishing were interrupted when the prefect was called back to Manaus for a conference with the governor. This was to include a visit with the prefect of the more-northerly reaches of the river at Erunepé. Combined with a week off to see his family again and uncertain flight schedules, *seu* Jader would be away from Guajará for at least two months. The only man who could stand in for him as prefect while he was gone was Adão. No one else was qualified.

Adão hated the idea of being prefect. Although the work would be easy—settling disputes, answering letters and generally loafing about—he would get more of the unwanted respect he had been trying to avoid. Now everybody would call him "*Senhor.*"

But, out of friendship and obligation, he accepted with a smile. "Of course," he said. "It will be the easiest job I've ever had. It's no imposition at all."

The next morning, *seu* Jader caught a canoe headed for Cruzeiro do Sul, loaded with chickens a farmer was taking to market. Adão was there to see him off. Oh, God, he thought. What am I going to say to people when they come to me with their problems? "Do what you see fit," the prefect had told him. That's all I can do, he thought. God!

That very first day, Dona Santa from next door came to him with a problem. Old Waldir's son, who was thirteen, had been following her youngest daughter, Suely, who was twelve, and was trying to kiss her. This had been going on for at least three days. "Can *O Senhor* do something about it?"

"Please. Just call me Adão. I'll talk to the boy about it. I'm sure he'll stop."

"Thank you so much. When *O Senhor* comes over for supper tonight, I'll have a special dessert for you."

"Please, Dona Santa, don't go to any trouble. It's my job. I'll be happy to do it."

The next day, *seu* Eduardo, the village tinsmith, candlemaker, and whitewasher, caught Adão as he walked past his tinwork. He had a problem.

"Your Honor, Dona Santa's cow rubbed her back on my new outhouse and knocked it over. It's a shambles. With her and her husband's money, they can surely afford a fence. Will you talk to them?"

"Please call me Adão, *seu* Eduardo. I'll talk to them, certainly. But everybody's cows wander all over town and no one has any barbed wire. Perhaps I will write a letter to the governor. He may send us some. I've heard that he's very generous."

"Thank you, your Honor. That's a wonderful idea. I'll make you some extra candles tonight."

"No, no. Please don't go to any trouble. It's only my job."

Then, there was the day two neighbors, Aureliano Vieira and Olmar Corrêa de Bulhões, got into a dispute over an orange tree that straddled their joint property line. "From what you've both just told me, and what you both agree on, is that you, Aureliano, planted the tree, and it has since grown over into your property, Olmar. And, from what you both have told me, you have shared equally the oranges over the last several years, and you, Olmar, always give Aureliano some extra melons from your field. Well, that sounds like a good agreement to me. I suspect that there's more behind this than you're telling me. But, if you must have an order from me, then my order is for you both to continue this arrangement until two years from now. At that time, the prefecture has plans to bring in surveyors in order to certify all boundary lines. Until then, I don't have enough information to help me make the best judgment."

Both men were happy with his decision, and both

offered Adão some oranges. He refused to accept any payment, but found two baskets full of the tasty fruit on his doorstep early the next morning.

These problem-solving chores luckily arose only once a day in a village the size of Guajará. On an exceptionally busy day there were two problems. Sometimes there were none. If it weren't for the fact that Adão would much prefer to be just another villager, he would have said he had a "*mamata*." A gravy job.

▼

The prefect's and Dona Santa's houses, along with three others, sat upon highlands within sight of the Juruá, but they all faced a small backwater that was a favorite anchorage for the small boats and canoes that plied the river. To get to the backwater from the houses, it was necessary to walk down the hill to the bottom lands, which were exposed during the dry season. Here, the river bottoms were extensive, creating a long one-hundred-yard walk from the high ground to the water's edge.

This was Adão's fishing spot. Although he ate Dona Santa's meals at state expense, he liked to help out. Being the one who handled the state's monies, he knew that they were often slow in paying their bills. This was mainly because of the red tape involved and the isolation of the region.

Other than being a good place to fish, it was peaceful. The cattle grazed here enough to keep the jungle away, but not often enough to destroy the beautiful green pastures they themselves had created. Here, too, was a haven from the ever-present mosquitoes and *piuns*. Only on a still day would they swarm and make folks miserable.

This morning, unable to sleep well, Adão had arisen before dawn, earlier than usual. Baiting his hook with worms he had dug up the night before, he already had a basket half full of fish by the time the sun started to rise. A good variety, he thought. Dona Santa will be pleased. Besides the plentiful piranhas and *mandins*, he had caught some striped catfish, two dog-fish, a *tucunaré* weighing about three pounds and a puffer fish called a *bacú*, which wasn't good to eat but made good fertilizer for gardens.

It was one of those mornings that he had never seen as a young man, growing up among the skyscrapers and multitudes of São Paulo. The sun was softly blowing rose colors into the puffy clouds floating above the three-family settlement of Príncipe, across the river. It drew from its timeworn bag of rainbows a magical green powder and cast it on the dark lands below. Hulking black shapes became trees. Darker black against lighter black became grass. Asleep became awake. Oblivion became

• • • • •

sleepy wonder. A dog barked, a cow mooed, and a monkey berated a small black squirrel for beating it to a tasty nut. Low overhead, a flock of parrots flew to welcome the new sun, their heads crimson with light, their tails yet black with night. Daily toil approached, with its tattered pockets full of sore backs and aching bodies.

Another day. An unsettling day.

Instead of marveling at this wonderful morning, Adão was preoccupied. He had been prefect for three weeks now. Everybody seemed to be satisfied with his few decisions. As usual, he had had no cross words with anyone. But something was definitely wrong. For the last two days, the villagers' attitude towards him had subtly changed. They were still friendly, still externally respectful, but were somehow more reserved. No one seemed to want to stop and pass the time of day. Prolonged conversations were nonexistent. It was always a cheerful wave of the hand and a *"Bom dia,"* or *"Como vai?"* Nothing but perfunctory greetings.

On his way down to the backwater he met Jurandyr de Mattos Galvão, a rubber tapper from Floresta. He told Adão that he knew of nothing happening in the village. But, then, he had only just now arrived and hadn't spoken to anyone. Adão thought that he wasn't telling the truth, but said nothing.

Maybe I've made some social error, he thought. Probably I've made some kind of wrong decision as prefect, and no one has told me about it. I wish I knew. Someone is coming this way. It looks like the policeman. It is. He'll tell me.

"*Seu* Aldyr, how are you this fine morning?"

"Just fine, your Honor," the usually taciturn man replied. From under shaggy gray eyebrows, he scowled at Adão, but in an almost too-friendly manner, he said, "That's a lot of fish you have there. You're a good fisherman. I'm going fishing too, but I prefer a net. Well, I'll see you later. I'm going to row over to the shallows across the river."

That's the most I've ever heard him say at one time, Adão thought. He's hiding something.

As the older man climbed hastily into his canoe, Adão asked, "*Seu* Aldyr, is something wrong? Everybody acts like something has happened."

"Nothing much ever happens around here. Eduardo's son, Nelson, fell from a tree yesterday and broke his wrist, and Moacyr and his wife had an argument last night. I heard that they were throwing things at each other. But when I got there they were already asleep. Until later," he said, making these his final words by pushing off from the shore with a crooked oar.

He's still talking too much, Adão thought. There's no doubt he's hiding something.

"*Seu* Aldyr . . . wait," he said. "Oh, never mind. I'll see you later."

Adão mulled over his neighbor's behavior. Folks who talk too much are barely speaking. Those who hardly ever speak are gabbing. I'm going to ask everybody I see until somebody tells me what is going on.

Here comes some woman running down the hill. It's not a woman. It's a girl. Wonderful. It's Dona Santa's daughter, Suely. We're good friends. She'll tell me.

Twelve-year-old Suely ran up to Adão, with her freshly ironed white dress flying—all sun-browned arms and legs—and her tousled hair aglow with early morning daylight.

"Adão," she said, breathless (besides the prefect, she was the only one in the village who called him Adão without first using a prefix), "my mother told me to ask you if she could bring your meals to you at your house. We're having company for a few days and there won't be room for everybody."

Hurt, but with a smile, Adão answered, "Of course. I don't mind."

"Adão, can I fish too?"

"If you want to. But you'll get your pretty dress dirty."

"Not if you bait the hook and take off the fish."

"I knew you would say that," he replied. "I'll let you fish if you'll answer a question for me."

"All right. What?"

"It seems like everybody has been hiding something from me, and now your mother doesn't want me in her house. Tell me why."

"But, *Mamãe* does want you in our house. It's just that we really are having company."

"Who is your company?"

"I'm not supposed to tell you."

"I see," Adão said, perplexed. Everyone *has* been hiding something. "Then everybody's not mad at me, Suely?"

"No, silly."

"Will you tell me what the secret is? I'll never tell anyone that you told me."

"*Tá.* I'll tell you my secret if you'll tell me one too."

"What kind of secret?"

"Any secret."

"Well . . . let me think. All right. *Seu* Jader snores so loudly that he keeps me awake. I've been able to sleep only since he's been gone."

"You silly, silly man. Everybody knows that he snores. Don't you remember? I live right next door. I've heard him myself. That's no secret. I want something serious."

Adão thought for a moment. "I think that everybody believes that I have a mysterious reason for coming to Guajará from São Paulo. If I tell you the real reason, would that be a good enough secret?"

"Oh, yes. Wonderful. I won't repeat it to anybody."

• • • • •

"Remember. Don't tell anyone at all."

"No one. Now hurry up and tell me."

"I came here . . . ah . . . I came here because I was engaged to a girl who . . . ran away with somebody else. This is as far away as I can get from what happened."

"Is that the truth?"

"Yes. I swear."

"I knew that was the reason. If someone comes here to live, it's always because they are running away from something. But, Adão, she must have been a very stupid girl. If I were older, and if I were your girlfriend, I'd stay with you. You're very nice. You never get angry with people."

"I do get angry. And, I'm going to get angry with you if you don't tell me your secret right away."

Suely stared into his face, her dark brown eyes meeting his lighter ones. "Do you like *curandeiros*?"

"*Curandeiros*!" he replied. "I don't know. I've never thought much about them. Do you mean those men who cure people with roots and herbs and things? I've heard that most of them are fakes."

"Our *curandeiro* isn't a fake. He truly does cure people."

"What does this have to do with me?" Adão asked.

"It's because the prefect doesn't like *curandeiros*. He told *seu* Estevão, our *curandeiro*, that he had to stop practicing in Guajará. He said that he would have the policeman arrest him if he disobeyed."

"Then, since I'm taking the prefect's place while he's gone, everybody thinks that I'll have the *curandeiro* arrested. Is that it?"

"Yes."

"And is he going to stay at your house?"

"Yes. He and his daughter and some other people."

"Why? Why are they staying there?"

"Because *seu* Estevão is going to hold a séance and an exorcism. Margarida, that's his daughter, has fits: she's possessed by a dead woman."

These softly spoken words—spoken with the naiveté of childhood, yet filled with knowledge of matters arcane and adult—troubled Adão and made him uneasy. He was relieved that the villagers were acting strangely, not because of him personally, but because of his temporary position as prefect. But the news that Guajará had a *curandeiro* was distressing.

Adão knew about *curandeiros*. Every small town in Brazil had one. Hundreds of them infested the larger cities, such as Rio de Janeiro and São Paulo. In fact they were prevalent not only in Brazil but all over South America, in Spanish-speaking countries as well. They were not unknown in North America and Europe. Yes, Adão knew about *curandeiros*. He remembered the one who had cured one of his aunts in São Paulo. He cured her of the cancer the doctors had told her was inoperable. The *curandeiro* had kneaded the flesh of her back and, after thirty minutes of this treatment, he had pulled the cancer from her body without even breaking the skin. The ugly, bloody mass he held in his hand was proof that she was cured forever. Truly a miracle. His aunt lived happily for two weeks after this treatment, and then died of the cancer the *curandeiro* had supposedly removed. The bloody mass he had taken from her body? A portion of a cow's liver slipped from his pocket by sleight of hand.

"Why are you so silent, Adão? Are you going to have the *curandeiro* arrested? Please don't. It will be my fault."

"No. I won't have him arrested. Don't worry. That wouldn't stop him because he's not really breaking any laws. But why is this happening in your house, Suely?"

"Because he lives too far back in the jungle."

"That's no answer," Adão said. "What does it matter where he lives?"

"When Margarida has a fit, she tries to run down to the river. She'll drown if she does that. *Seu* Estevão has tried to keep her tied to her bed, but she rubs sores on her arms and legs, trying to get away, and since our house is the biggest one in town, enough people can watch her and grab her if she tries to leave. Don't you see? She's very strong when she's possessed. It takes at least four grown men to hold her down. And since her real mother is dead, my mother helps tend her when she's calm. I help, too. We try to get her to eat and drink, and we give her baths."

"That's terrible!"

"Yes, it is. And scary, too."

"Don't worry," Adão said. "I might look into this, but I won't tell anybody that you told me.

"Come on," he said. "You wanted to fish. Let's think of happier things."

"Let's."

God. What a quandary, he thought. It was so different back in São Paulo. Being in Guajará is like being back in some darker age. Possession by ghosts. Candles instead of electricity. No doctors . . . well, I'll think about it later. And I thought I was happy here!

▼

By late afternoon of the same day that Suely had told him about the *curandeiro*, Adão had decided to feign ignorance for the time being. Perhaps the ghost would be exorcised by tonight, and everything could get back to normal.

After a filling, tasty supper of fried pork and potatoes, and a dessert of plump mangoes, Adão felt too lazy to

• • • • •

leave the house that night. He was looking forward to reading a good mystery story that he had not yet unpacked from his suitcase. Maybe I can get my mind off of these unhappy matters, he thought.

Dona Santa had brought him his meal, but it was Suely who came back to pick up the dishes. From her he learned more about the exorcism and the inexplicable events which had preceded it.

As far back as anyone could remember, Guajará had had only one other case of spirit possession. It was ten years ago. A young woman, the mother of two small children, had become seriously ill with fever. For days she had lain in bed and had finally shown signs of recovering when, late one night, she began muttering incomprehensible things about having lived a previous life. According to her husband and a neighbor, she had spoken in an unfamiliar voice and told them that her name in her former life was Isabel, and that she had been miserable with a husband who often beat her and who gave her no children. After giving this small amount of intelligible information, she began to babble in a strange language. Later, she started to speak of going to the river where it was warm; where she, the ghost, now was, it was unbearably cold. Shortly thereafter, before anyone could stop her, the woman leaped through the window, ran down to the river, and jumped in. Presumably she had drowned. Her body was never found.

According to Suely, the *curandeiro*'s daughter, Margarida, was possessed by the same ghost. She not only wanted to run down to the river and throw herself in, she spoke with the same voice as had the other possessed woman, and called herself by the same name, Isabel.

Ever since Margarida was small she had had seizures of some kind, but they only lasted for a moment, and with days between occurrences. At worst, she would fall to the ground and roll around. At the mildest, she would stare blankly for less than a minute, not seeing or hearing anything that was happening around her. This time she was ill with a fever when she had a seizure and, as the *curandeiro* explained it, in her weakened condition she had become prey for the malevolent dead woman.

Adão was not a religious man. Still, he wasn't quite an atheist. He had yet to see proof that there was no God. On occasion he did go to church, but mainly because he enjoyed the ceremonies. For this reason he didn't want to consider this problem in a religious light. Also, superstitiously, he couldn't consider it. He was afraid of the unknown but looked for rationales.

To Adão, the sad events of ten years ago were obviously not a case of spirit possession at all; only a feverish woman who thought that she was someone else. Hallucinations keep apace with heavy fevers as they rise and fall.

Although he knew very little about medicine and diseases, the present case of Margarida was easily explainable by other than supernatural means. She probably was epileptic. This, combined with her fever and her undoubted knowledge of the other woman's seeming possession, was the cause of her delusions. There could be no other explanation.

The only thing that really bothered him was the fact that the villagers could believe in such things. True, most of them could neither read nor write, and even fewer of them knew much of the outside world, but after getting to know them as well as any stranger could in just a few short months, he found them intelligent, industrious, and practical.

The belief in ghosts can be contagious, he thought. I'll keep an open mind, but I won't fall into that trap. Anyway, this can't go on much longer.

Settling back in the prefecture's only chair, propping his legs over the prefecture's only desk, and lighting one of *seu* Eduardo's candles, Adão opened the unread mystery and tried to blot out his troublesome thoughts. After thirty minutes of only half understanding what he was reading, he put the book down. Murmuring coming

• • • • •

from Dona Santa's house would break into his mind no matter how hard he tried to ignore it. Only an old orange tree separated the two houses.

To get away, he picked up his book and candle and went to the back room. He unrolled his hammock from where it hung on a hook set in the wall and stretched it to a hook on the other wall. Since all the windows were unshuttered, he snuffed out the candle and undressed in the dark. After lying down in the hammock and pulling a cover over his body to keep out the chill of the night air, he re-lit the candle and set it on the windowsill. The murmuring, less distinct now but still intrusive, continued to bother him. It's no good, he thought with disgust. I can still hear them.

Again he blew out the candle and lay back, trying to get his thoughts in order. Bright moonlight peeked over a cloud and flooded the room with half-light. On the ceiling were the two resident geckoes of the house. On spindly legs and with white lizard's bodies, they danced prettily back and forth, chasing the insects that Adão's candle had attracted into the room. As they ran in and out of the moon's glow, they changed from pale, recognizable beings into even paler wraiths, sometimes disappearing into dark shadows.

The gleefully prancing geckoes, the indistinct voices droning from next door, and the soft ethereal moonlight combined to lull Adão to the edge of sleep. He had just about lost consciousness when a loud bang and a scuffling noise shocked him awake. It came from Dona Santa's house. The voices were louder. Words became distinct and understandable.

A chill played down the back of his neck. Shadows moved. A black, man-like shape stood near the foot of his hammock.

God! he thought. Who is it?

Oh . . . hell! It's only my clothes hanging on the wall. Now I'll never get to sleep. I'd better see what is going on.

After arising from his hammock and pulling on his pants, Adão walked in the dark to the front of the house. Knowing that he was spying, and feeling guilty for it, he nevertheless looked into Dona Santa's open front-room window, directly across from his own.

The wind had started blowing and had begun to softly whistle through the eaves. The orange tree's branches noisily scraped against the side of the house.

From the window opposite came a bright yellow light, shining as if many candles were lit. Only light. Silence. From inside a hand gripped the window sill. An old hand. The top of someone's head appeared. Gray hair. Old hair. Suddenly they vanished, leaving again only the bright light.

• • • • •

Now voices. Prayers battling for clarity with the sound of the wind and the rustling branches. Fading in and out like some distant radio station.

One voice. Old, deep: "... *nome do Pai e do Filho e ...*"

Many voices: "... *bendita sois ... as mulheres ... rogai por nos ...*"

One voice. Old, deep: "... *do Filho e do Espirito ...*"

Many voices: "*Nosso Pai ...*"

One voice. A girl's voice, muttering.

The wind won the battle. It increased in force, becoming louder, sweeping clouds across the night sky. The voices became again their now familiar indistinct murmur.

Adão left the window and went back to his hammock, his book, and his candle, determined to read until he fell asleep.

Resisting recurring impulses to look over his shoulder, he forced himself to concentrate on the book. The next thing he knew, the sun was shining rosily through the window, his book was lying open on his chest, and the candle had become a waxy nothing.

▼

That morning Suely brought him a breakfast of a pot of coffee and some fried bananas. He could tell by the shadows under her eyes that she hadn't slept well.

"Good morning, Adão."

"Good morning. You look sleepy. How is Margarida?"

"The same. I don't think that the *curandeiro* will ever get rid of that ghost. It's frightening. Do you think that it will get inside of me?"

Seeing how worried she was, Adão hastily reassured her. "No. Of course not. I'm 100 percent positive that it won't."

Why did I say it like that, he thought. I'm speaking as if it really is a ghost.

"My mother is sending all of us younger children across the river to spend the night with my aunt. She said that she didn't realize that it would take so long a time for the exorcism."

"I know that it will be over soon," he replied. "But I'm glad that you aren't staying there tonight. Suely, will you ask your mother to come over here when she gets a chance? I don't think that I should go over to your house just yet."

"*Tá.* I'll ask her. She'll be here anyway to get the dishes."

As she headed for the door, Adão said, "Suely. Don't worry. Nothing will happen. I promise."

"Adão. Your blessing?"

Touched that she should ask his blessing, he replied, "God bless you. Remember. Don't worry."

▼

With perfect unplanned timing, Dona Santa knocked on the door just as he finished the last of the coffee.

"Come in."

"*Bom dia, seu* Adão. Did you wish to speak to me?"

Adão noticed shadows under her eyes also. Dona Santa was a slender woman. Still young in years, but aging prematurely because of her life of constant work at home and in her family's fields of corn and sugar cane. A very intelligent person, Adão thought. How can she let something like this happen in her house?

"Yes. I did want to see you, Dona Santa. As you know, the prefect has put me in charge while he is gone. Well . . . here I am, going into a long, pompous speech. I just want to say that I know all about the *curandeiro* and what's happening at your house."

"Did Suely tell you?" she asked, with an astuteness that surprised Adão.

"No. Not at all," he lied. "I can't help but hear what's going on at your house. Also, I've asked around and have learned the whole story."

"Are you going to have *seu* Aldyr arrest the *curandeiro*?" Lines of worry crossed her face and concern was in her voice.

"No. Why should I? There's no doctor here and the *curandeiro* is all Margarida has. Besides, he is her father. I'm sure that he is doing his best. And, besides that, I'm only a temporary prefect appointed by another temporary prefect. I don't think that my position is strictly legal."

Smiling now, Dona Santa asked, "Will you come over tonight? I'll tell the *curandeiro* what you said. Maybe you can help."

"I can't do anything. I'm not a doctor. But I will come. I suppose that since I'm in charge of the village, I should at least know what is happening firsthand."

"Thank you, *seu* Adão. You're such a good man."

"No, I'm not. But I'll be there."

▼

The day passed rapidly. Too rapidly for Adão. He had second thoughts about going to the exorcism.

He walked to his land through the jungle path which bordered the river and spent the day talking to his nearest neighbor. His neighbor was old Sebastião, the town's only black and its only leper. For lunch they shared some oranges and some bananas Dona Santa had packed for him.

By nightfall he was back at the prefecture, dreading the idea of going next door.

▼

Dona Santa's sturdy old house seemed saddened by the events transpiring within. It watched Adão as he stood hesitant on the steps leading to its insides. Maybe he can make things happy again.

What can I do? Adão thought. Nothing. Why should I be here?

Voices grew quiet when he stepped through the doorway. He glanced briefly around the room. In it were two long makeshift benches and some of the handmade chairs common to this region. In the far corner was a bed. In the chairs and sitting on the benches were about fifteen or twenty people, most of whom he already knew. There was Dona Santa; *seu* Bonifacio; the policeman, *seu* Aldyr; and Moacyr Velho, the owner of the *botequim.* The others were farmers and fishermen. Two were strangers, local men who spent most of their time in the jungle hunting for animal hides.

Many candles were lit, and the air was filled with heavy blue smoke from home-grown tobacco rolled into coarse cigarettes or stuffed into roughly carved pipes. The latter were smoked mainly by the women.

The heat was oppressive: not usual for this time of year, since Guajará was farther south and at a higher elevation than most of the rest of Amazonas. Oppressive, too, were the mosquitoes, which were unusually numerous this far from the river. They industriously plied their trade in the hot, still air, finding a plenitude of warm blood.

Adão remembered this room fondly, as it had been before. There was once a supper table in the middle and a foot-operated sewing machine in the corner, where the bed was now. He remembered the many meals he had eaten here, and the long friendly conversations he had had with Dona Santa, *seu* Bonifacio, and their children. He recalled telling them about far-away São Paulo, and their telling him about Guajará and the latest gossip. The changes wrought within the room made the exorcism more believable, more serious. Here were grown people, adults, who believed that a girl had actually been possessed by a malign spirit. No wonder Suely had been so frightened.

As he looked around the room, everyone nodded or smiled in recognition. No one spoke until Dona Santa came to him.

"*Seu* Adão. Come. I want you to meet our *curandeiro.*"

They crossed the room to the bed where an old, gray-haired man knelt, his hand on the hand of his sleeping daughter.

The *curandeiro* arose to his feet and Dona Santa introduced them. "*Muito prazer,*" the *curandeiro* said, taking Adão's hand.

"*Prazer,*" Adão returned with a smile.

The *curandeiro* was probably the oldest man in Guajará. He was seventy-nine—long-lived for these forgotten lands. Craggy-featured and stoop-shouldered with age, he was probably the poorest man in the village as well. His clothes had been patched many times. Even some of the patches had been patched. He habitually went barefooted, as did many of his fellow townsfolk. Whenever he went to the city of Cruzeiro do Sul, he usually dipped his feet in a vat of the hot latex which had come from the local rubber trees, coming away with instant shoes that lasted the day through.

Yet, as poor as he was, by fishing and an occasional carpentry job he always managed to provide shoes and clothes for his seventeen children, all of whom, with the exception of Margarida, had grown up and left home. Margarida, at sixteen, was his youngest.

Adão found that the *curandeiro*, though aged, still had a firm handshake, and his voice was steady. Only his eyes were truly old. They had that intangible cloudiness that sometimes comes late in life.

"Dona Santa told me that you understand what I'm trying to do," the *curandeiro* said. "I had hoped that you would. As you can see, my daughter is very ill."

Turning to face the bed, something that he had been avoiding, Adão could see the truth of the *curandeiro*'s words. Although sleeping now, with freshly combed hair and clean clothes, he saw that she was terribly emaciated. Her lips were parched and her once-lovely arms and legs were covered with bruises. The bruises, he was told, had been unwillingly caused by the men who had to hold her down whenever she tried to leave the house and run down to the river.

Glancing from her face to her bruise-covered body and back again to her face took only the smallest part of a second. When again Adão looked at Margarida's face, he was stunned to find her staring at him with bright, feverish eyes. He found that he couldn't move. Her gaze was hypnotic, filled with malice, wrath, and (did he only imagine it?) a touch of fear.

Slowly her eyes lost their focus. Softening, they looked away. Weakly she pleaded, "Please. Someone bring me some water. I'm so thirsty."

While Adão stood dumbfounded, Dona Santa walked hurriedly back to her kitchen and returned with a tin cup, which she then filled with water by dipping it into an earthenware pot. She handed this to the *curandeiro,* who, with a slightly shaky hand, raised Margarida's head and gave her small sips of the soothing liquid.

Dona Santa motioned to Adão to sit beside her at the foot of the bed. As soon as he had sat down, he looked back towards Margarida. She was again staring at him. He could feel the anger she directed towards him. Suddenly, she bent her neck forward and clamped her teeth on the tin cup, pulling it from the *curandeiro*'s hand and spilling it over her throat and down her dress.

For long moments she held his eyes with her own,

the rim of the tin cup firmly between her teeth. Adão wondered why no one moved to take the cup away from her.

As if reading his thoughts, the *curandeiro* turned to him to explain. "We don't try to remove the cup since we have to force her jaws open and it will do more harm to her than the cup will. She does this all the time. I don't know why she keeps on staring at you. Until now, she's always avoided looking people directly in the eyes."

The *curandeiro* turned towards his daughter, blocking her view of Adão. Instantly the cup fell to the floor and she began to speak.

"How are you, old man? Are you going to let me take your daughter down to the river tonight?"

Adão knew from watching horror movies and from hearsay that now was the time for the *curandeiro* to bring forth a cross, since demons were supposed to be afraid of them. All *curandeiros* and priests used crosses in the exorcisms. I wonder what he is going to do, he thought.

The next thing the *curandeiro* did was to take a heavy wooden cross from his pocket, lowering himself in the eyes of Adão. Yet, what has he to gain by this? he considered. No one in Guajará has money. The man must be a quack, but this is his own daughter. Surely he can see that she is hallucinating. She needs to be taken in to Cruzeiro.

· · · · ·

"Not that damned cross again," the girl on the bed said. "It's such a disgusting thing. Do you want to make your daughter sicker than she already is?"

With the cross, the *curandeiro* made several passes over the girl's prone body and began to recite the Lord's prayer. When he began his prayers, he moved slightly, unblocking Margarida's view of Adão. This time she didn't stare at him. She caught his eyes for only a moment before turning quickly away, as if she were somehow afraid of him. From that point on, she refused to speak.

For over thirty minutes the *curandeiro* said prayers and invoked the name of Jesus to drive out the dead woman's soul from his daughter. Her only reaction was one of fear; recoiling from the cross as it came near. When it was placed directly on her, her entire body would tremble. But she was completely silent.

Finally old Estevão left the bedside and sat down in a chair. His head was bowed with weariness. His efforts were having little effect.

Dona Santa whispered to Adão, "Your presence is affecting Margarida. She's never acted like this before now."

Ever since Adão first walked through the door, mixed feelings had been hammering away at his armor of disbelief—feelings of fear, wonder, anger, pity, and shock. But they had succeeded only in making a tiny opening. He replied to Dona Santa, "Maybe I'd best leave." After a pause, he said, "I'll see you tomorrow. Please let me know how she is doing."

He arose and left the house, saying nothing more, only nodding to *seu* Bonifacio, who said, "Good night," as he passed by.

▼

Adão stood silently facing the river. It was almost visible in the bright light from the full moon. His mind was a blank. He had an uneasy feeling that he had somehow become irrevocably involved in the horror that had taken up residence in Dona Santa's house.

Adão had always been an undecided person in his beliefs. Politically he was neither leftist nor rightist, nor even somewhere in between. It was just that he owned his own mind when it came to thoughts about the rightness or wrongness of things, not a borrower of the many-celled, labyrinthine mind of dogma. His usual answer when asked about his ideas or thoughts about any of the unsolved mysteries of life was "I don't know." Yet, regardless of this indecisiveness in his beliefs, he did not vacillate when circumstances demanded an answer. His decisions were delayed and considered, if delay was possible. But if circumstances demanded an instant decision, he could make one faster than most people.

• • • • •

Here, though, was a dilemma. He knew that the prefect would be upset with him when he returned. But he had no real authority to interfere with the *curandeiro*. And why should he? He wasn't omnipotent. Anything he might try to do for Margarida could easily do her less benefit than it would harm. He couldn't kidnap her and take her into Cruzeiro do Sul.

After much thought, he saw that there was little he could do. If she hadn't improved by tomorrow, he decided that his only course of action would be to talk to the doctor in Cruzeiro. Perhaps he could come here to Guajará, or at least prescribe some kind of medicine.

▼

There was little use in trying to sleep. Behind him he could hear the prayers starting again. At least for a while he needed to get away from the unhappy house next door. The moon was bright enough for him to see his way without a candle or flashlight. He would walk down to the backwater.

Here there was peace. He sat on the soft grass with his legs hanging over the embankment. Barely discernable were the eyes of a small caiman, shining from the far shore. Tiny frogs made plopping sounds as they jumped in and out of the water, seeking even tinier insects. A fish splashed further out in the middle of the river.

The river, Margarida, the dead woman—the train of thought brought back unbidden a picture of the exorcism. Unconsciously his hand went to the small golden cross on the thin chain around his neck. It was a cross that his mother had given him in the vain hope that it would bring him back to the church.

Why did she stare at me so intensely? he asked himself. Why me and no one else? If there really is a dead woman's ghost inside Margarida, why is she so obsessed with the river? It's probably cold, not warm like she says it is.

Without thinking, he reached down to feel the water. Then, with startling clarity, came the thought: Why did I come down to this very river? What am I doing here?

At the same moment, instead of touching the water, he touched the slick back of a passing mud turtle, causing him to sit back too rapidly.

A muffled scream and a furry something behind his back brought him instantly to his feet.

"Oh you stupid cat. You nearly gave me a heart attack. If you had given me warning, I wouldn't have sat on you."

Bending down to pet the cat, Adão glanced around, hoping that no one had seen what had happened. "You must be Fatima's cat, Bom Jesus. What is that you have there in your mouth? Is it a bird?"

• • • • •

Knowing that you can't usually get a bird from a cat's mouth without first choking it nearly to death, Adão held out his hand and said, with little hope of success, "Let me see it."

Surprisingly, Bom Jesus came up to him and dropped the bird into his hand. "Why did you do that, Bom Jesus? Cats don't give people birds. Do you want me to look at it?"

It was a *Mãe-da-lua*, a mother-of-the-moon, one of those lovely nightjars with a mouth almost as big as its body. "Well, it's still alive and its wings aren't broken. I don't need another mystery. Do you want me to fix it?"

Adão stared into Bom Jesus's friendly, deep blue eyes. "If I were superstitious, I'd believe that this is an omen. Come on, cat. If Dona Santa's cow is close by, I'll get you some milk."

That night, Bom Jesus, with a stomach full of milk, slept with Adão in his hammock. Adão slept fitfully, being plagued with nightmares, and the *Mãe-da-lua* flew off the window sill into the early morning sky, swearing to never again fly without looking where she was going. She still had a headache from banging into *seu* Eduardo's new outhouse.

▼

The next day, Adão borrowed *seu* Aldyr's boat with its new "*Burro Preito*" motor and left for Cruzeiro do Sul. The long trip gave him time to think, but he could

• • • • •

come up with no workable answers. Soon he contented himself with watching for large caimans on the occasional sandy beaches or slowing down to avoid running into playful fresh-water dolphins.

In Cruzeiro, he encountered Edison Graça, a farmer from Guajará, whom he seldom saw, since he and his family lived far back in the jungle. Over coffee in a small, one-room café in the middle of the market, Graça gave him directions to the doctor's office and the church. He and Adão found common ground in that they both had been unable to sleep well since the exorcism had begun. Both hoped that it would end soon.

Everyone was sympathetic, but no one could help. The doctor said that he would be glad to treat Margarida if Adão would bring her in. He couldn't leave because he had too many people to take care of in Cruzeiro. He did give Adão some strong aspirins.

The priests said that they would be glad to come, but in cases like this, the villagers always spirited away the *curandeiros* and their charges. Father Vicente was due to go next week anyway. He was to hold services in the small chapel the townsfolk had built for him and Father O'Malley. He would look into the matter then. "Seldom do people die from these misguided exorcisms," he said. "We can give you some aspirin and some good medicine we have for fevers. Make sure that she takes some."

The German nuns at the convent school gave him

some pills for infections and some aspirin. One of them promised to leave with Father Vicente when he went to Guajará.

The pharmacist sold him a panacea, which Adão knew was useless, but, who knows? Maybe it would work. Straws were there for the grasping. Why not?

An orderly at the maternity clinic gave him some good advice and a half-pint bottle of aspirin.

Dejected, Adão headed back to Guajará, arriving just in time to give Dona Santa some of the medicine and instructions on how to use it, before the next attempt at an exorcism began.

▼

That night he wearily walked the path to his land, finding a good spot clear of fallen underbrush in which to sleep away his problems. He did have a good sleep. Nothing interrupted his lost dreams. A passing mother opossum, with her tiny babies clinging to her rough fur, ran away in fright. A paca, a coati, a deer, and a mouse all came by to see him, but passed stealthily on.

The next morning, Adão arrived at Dona Santa's house, but didn't enter. He spoke to her through the window. No, he was told. The medicine didn't help, but the *curandeiro* was pleased that Adão had taken an interest in helping. They would try the medicine again today.

Adão began to spend all his nights at his land. Every

morning he would come in to eat breakfast and inquire after Margarida. The answer was always the same. "Nothing seems to help, *seu* Adão. The poor thing is just wasting away. She won't eat anything. She's much worse."

The fourth day after his return from Cruzeiro do Sul, he decided to see for himself how Margarida was faring–if, he thought, remembering how she had stared at him, he could gather enough courage to go through that now-unfriendly doorway.

Upon entering the house, he found that it wasn't such a terrible place after all. The bright morning sun almost, but not quite, made the room seem cheerful. But when he saw the body of the pallid, sick creature lying in the bed, the sunlight vanished from his consciousness. Margarida was so thin that her dress no longer fit, serving only to cover the many bruises and scratches, more numerous than they had been when Adão had first seen her.

There were the usual four men in the room. They were sitting quietly beside the bed. He knew all of them. There was Moacyr Velho, *seu* Bonifacio, *seu* Aldyr, and Zé Maia, *seu* Bonifacio's oldest son. The only other person in the room besides the four men and Margarida was an old woman who sat in the corner by herself, sound asleep.

Sitting down next to *seu* Bonifacio, Adão asked in a low voice, "How is she today?"

Seu Bonifacio replied, "Much, much worse. She's been raving and saying terrible things all night. Four times . . . no, five times, she tried to jump out of bed. It's a lucky thing that we were able to hold her down in the bed instead of wrestling with her on the floor. She can't use any more bruises."

What's another bruise or two, Adão thought, instantly surprised at himself for thinking so cynically.

Everyone sat in silence for about twenty minutes. The only sounds were everyday ones from outside, and the soft breathing coming from the bed.

An urgent need to smoke a cigarette overpowered him. Luckily the cigarette *seu* Bonifacio handed him was a store-bought one instead of the strong local variety. He hadn't smoked for the last four years, and was almost overcome by a fit of coughing. A stronger one would probably have made him sick.

Margarida awoke, glanced at Adão, then went back to sleep.

Feeling embarrassed, he was wondering to himself about why, of all things, he should want a cigarette, when pandemonium erupted.

Margarida leapt from the bed, heading straight for Adão. The fast-thinking Zé Maia grabbed her ankle and brought her to the floor. Instantly, all four men jumped on top of her struggling body. They attempted to hold her down and at the same time avoid her raking fingernails and her sharp teeth.

Adão stood up, ready to help if needed, but, fortunately, the pitiful girl fainted, bringing relief to all involved.

Seu Aldyr and Moacyr Velho picked her up by her arms and legs and, not too gently it seemed to Adão, put her back in the bed. Moacyr Velho turned to him and said, apologetically, "What else can we do?"

Everyone, including Adão, sat back down. No one said a word, being either too weary or too upset to do so. For five minutes they sat thus. All during this time an unreasonable, uncontrollable anger grew in Adão's breast. Anger at the well-meaning men who had undoubtedly injured Margarida by piling on top of her. Anger at himself for being so inept. Anger at Margarida for allowing herself to be so deluded. Anger at the malign spirit, if, of course, there could be such an unlikely thing in the first place.

Unthinkingly, only vaguely aware of anything else in the room but the sick girl in the bed, Adão walked up to her and bent over. Her eyes were open but averted, staring at nothing.

What he did next was to cure Margarida forever of her delusion and/or evil spirit.

Where it had taken the *curandeiro* many days and

• • • • •

nights of unsuccessful attempts at an exorcism, along with the futile help of most of the villagers, and the equally futile medicines and panaceas brought from Cruzeiro do Sul by Adão himself, it took Adão but the briefest of moments to prevent Margarida's death, which was sure to come had he not acted.

Up and down the river, for many years afterwards, friendly arguments abounded because there were many varying opinions as to what had actually happened. The old woman who had been in the room had slept through the whole thing, tired from watching Margarida all night long. But she swore that she had seen in a dream a devil staring through the window at the events happening within, this at the very moment the dead woman's ghost had fled from Margarida. Moacyr Velho swore that he felt a chilling wind pass him by as something invisible hurriedly left the room through the open doorway.

Adão, if he could be persuaded to talk about it, refused to admit that he had done anything at all, but secretly felt that he knew what had really happened. When Margarida had become sick with fever and subsequently began to have delusions, it became necessary to have an exorcism. Whether there was an evil spirit actually living inside her, whether she was only hallucinating, it made no difference. The effect of an exorcism would be the same. It would drive away either the ghost or the delusion, whichever was the case.

But, since it was most probably a delusion and nothing more, the exorcism had, for some unknown reason, become in itself the sickness. It had somehow passed the point where it would cure her, veering away to become that which only prolonged everything. Seeing that everyone in town, including her own father, unshakably believed that she was truly possessed, and knowing that demons were afraid of crosses, prayers, and all the rites of exorcism, she couldn't help but act out the role that was expected of her. Her fears of the exorcism were very real fears indeed. It was only when Adão came to take away those fears that she could once again enter the land of reality.

Surprisingly, the *curandeiro*'s theory ran almost parallel to that of Adão's private thoughts, except that he placed more emphasis on an evil spirit.

What Adão did was a very sacrilegious thing. A very simple thing. A very brief nothing of a thing.

When he approached Margarida's bed that sunshiny morning, his anger was apparent to the other four men in the room. All four stood up, not sure if they should protect Margarida from Adão or Adão from Margarida.

With a steady, deeper than usual voice, angrily, he turned to *seu* Bonifacio and asked, "Can she understand me?"

"Yes."

"Are you sure?"

"Yes. Positive."

Turning back to Margarida, bending closer to her face, he asked, "Can you hear me?"

"Yes."

"You're sure?"

"Yes."

Reaching into his shirt and withdrawing from it the golden cross his mother had given him so long ago, he asked, "Do you see this?"

"Yes," she answered, her voice quivering with fear.

"You're sure? You do see this cross?"

"Yes." Puzzlement seemed added to the fear she felt.

Almost yelling it in her face, he said, "It doesn't mean a thing!" Whereupon he tore the cross from his neck and angrily threw it out the window.

That's all he did. A very brief nothing of a thing.

He glared at the other men, then stalked from the room, fury still confusing his thoughts.

Once outside, embarrassment flooded his entire being. How could I do such a thing? he thought. Now I've only made things worse. Oh, what an idiot I am!

He went directly to his land and stayed there for two days, ashamed to talk to anyone.

If only he had stayed one moment longer at Dona Santa's house. He would have heard, coming from the bed, "Why did he do that? I'm so hungry. Can someone bring me something to eat?"

* * * * *

Was there a ghost or was it a delusion? Pay heed to a wise man. Ask Adão. Most of his answer would be interesting and should be listened to with respect, although it will undoubtedly be fraught with *if*s, *but*s, *possibly*s, and *may* or *may not*s. But listen to his first three words.

Pay heed to a wise man. He will say, "I don't know."

Epilogue

The first hint that Adão had that he had cured Margarida instead of making her condition worse was early in
the morning of the second day after he had left the town
in shame.

He was sifting through his fingers the fine ashes that
were left over from the all-consuming inferno that his
land had become the night before after he had set fire
to the brush he had cleared all summer. It had been a

spectacular blaze. The glow on the horizon could be seen as far south as Cruzeiro do Sul, and as far north as the river town of Boa Fé at the confluence of the Juruá and the Rio Ipixuna. All that was left were a few of the larger logs he had felled, still smoldering, some still ablaze.

Hearing a noise behind him he looked back and found the leper, old Sebastião, standing there.

"*Bom dia, seu* Adão. That was a wonderful fire. I was a little worried that it might spread to my house."

"Oh, Sebastião, I'm so sorry. I didn't think."

"No, no. Don't apologize. My house is all right. I was worrying over nothing. Ah, *seu* Adão. Can you do me a favor?"

"Of course. Anything."

"I've never asked this of anybody until now. Usually Dona Santa or Dona Pipira or the *curandeiro* do it, but . . . just once, could you do it? Just once?"

"Do what?"

Hesitant, pausing for a long time before again speaking, Sebastião blurted out, "Change the wrappings on my hands. I've got some cloth at home but I can't do it myself. My fingers are almost gone. I wouldn't ask you but you do eat at my house and you once felt my forehead when you thought I had a fever . . . but, no. I shouldn't ask. I—"

Butting in, Adão replied, "I'll be very happy to do it. Come on. Let's go to your house and do it now."

Strange, Adão thought as they walked the short distance to Sebastião's hovel. Why is he asking me to do this?

After changing Sebastião's bandages and relaxing with a hot cup of coffee the old leper had brewed for him, he heard the story of how he had cured Margarida.

At first, he was swept by a feeling of elation. Margarida was cured and the exorcism was over. Too, he could return to town without shame. But horror pushed elation aside when he realized why old Sebastião wanted him to change his bandages.

"Sebastião," he said, his voice barely hiding the compassion and guilt he felt. "I hope that you don't think that I can cure your leprosy. Is that why you wanted me to help you? I didn't cure Margarida; or if I did, it was accidental. I don't even know why I did what I did."

"The *curandeiro* was right," the old man replied. "He said that you have a lot of power, only you don't realize it."

The *curandeiro* again, Adão thought. At least he doesn't seem to be upset with me.

"I try to be realistic," Sebastião continued. "I know that I can't be cured. The *curandeiro* told me so. He said that he would try to get me into a sanitarium, but

I'd rather stay here with my friends." (Maybe the *curandeiro* wasn't such a charlatan after all.) "But, Adão, please forgive me. Sometimes I have these useless hopes. . . ."

"I wish that I could do something," Adão said. "But I really can't. Every time I'm out here, though, I'll check on you. I don't mind changing your bandages. Not at all."

Walking back to town, he tried to banish from his mind the undeserved sense of guilt he felt about old Sebastião. *There's nothing I can do. I just won't think about it. I hope that no one else wants me to cure them. Maybe he'll be the only one.*

He was wrong.

For the next two weeks everything had almost gotten back to normal. Normal—except that now respect was written on everyone's face. Written with a large brush. Even the cows and chickens seemed to defer to him.

He was taking his meals again at Dona Santa's house. The front room was as it was before. There was no sign of the exorcism. It was a happy house again.

Seu Estevão, the *curandeiro*, was profuse with his thanks and gratitude. He even asked Adão to become the new *curandeiro* for Guajará. He was getting old and couldn't handle the job much longer. He would be willing to teach him all about the different herbs he used for hookworms, colds, wounds, and minor illnesses. He told Adão that he never tried to treat cancers or other diseases that were best left in the hands of a doctor. But somebody had to take care of the villagers. At least for their minor problems.

Adão politely refused to become the next *curandeiro*, but he grew fond of the old man. *Seu* Estevão not only helped the townsfolk with their sicknesses, he also helped them to write their letters, and he read the responses they received. He was everywhere. Always doing something for somebody, always without receiving payment, except possibly a good supper at times.

He became friends, too, with Margarida. She was rapidly regaining her health and was beginning to look pretty again. For some reason, inexplicable even to themselves, neither she nor Adão ever mentioned the exorcism to each other.

There were more problems for him to solve as prefect, twice as many as before. There was now a new element added to his daily chores.

One day, *seu* Aldyr came up to him and asked, "Your Honor, I've been having some awful back pains. Would you know of something that might help?"

He answered, "I really know nothing about medicine, *seu* Aldyr. I can give you some aspirins. If they don't help, then you should see the *curandeiro*, or see the doctor in Cruzeiro."

"Thank you so much, your honor. I know that the aspirins will help."

The next day an old woman from the jungle caught Adão down at his fishing spot.

"Your Honor, I have these terrible pains in my head. I've heard that you can cure them. Will you help me?"

"Oh, no, *Senhora*. I don't know how to cure people. I'm not a doctor . . . or a *curandeiro*. I do have plenty of aspirins. If you will go to the prefecture, you'll find some in the back room. Take a handful. No. Take two handfuls. And use them sparingly."

"Thank you, your Honor. *O Senhor* is a great man."

Adão resigned himself to what was happening around him. If I continue to refuse to treat people, they'll gradually stop, he thought. This can't go on forever.

The following day, he was returning from a visit with old Sebastião, whose bandages he had changed, when, upon approaching the prefecture, he noticed Dona Santa standing in its doorway talking to a tall, slender woman—one he had never seen before.

As he came nearer, he saw a third woman, a younger one, looking out of the prefecture's window. Adão's heartbeat speeded up. What a lovely, lovely girl, he thought. What lovely brown hair. It must reach to her waist.

Adão smiled at her as he walked up. She didn't smile back. Nonplussed, he wondered about his appearance. Maybe she's looking over my head at the river and didn't notice me, he thought. I hope I haven't done something wrong.

"*Seu* Adão," Dona Santa said. "I'm glad that you came back so early. Two of my relatives from Boa Fé stopped by on their way back from Cruzeiro. They wanted to talk to you."

Dona Santa introduced them as *Senhora* de Melo and her niece Janina. *Senhora* de Melo was the schoolteacher in Boa Fé.

This time, the girl in the window smiled back at him. Adão found himself entranced by her eyes. They were the same deep blue color as those of Bom Jesus. He had to force himself to look away. He had become totally, irreversibly captivated. It was something that had never happened to him before.

He hardly heard Dona Santa when she made an excuse to leave them in order to help her husband in the fields. He nodded in numb agreement when *Senhora* de Melo asked him if they could go inside so that she might speak to him.

Once they were inside with Janina, *Senhora* de Melo

• • • • •

began to talk, but Adão only halfway understood what she was saying. Not daring to look at Janina, but aware of her presence as he had never been aware of another person, he had to struggle with himself to try to be the attentive prefect they had come to see.

Senhora de Melo's words began to break into his consciousness. ". . . realistic. We both know that it is useless, but we can't let even the smallest chance go by."

Realistic? Useless? What is she talking about? I must pay attention, he thought, daring to glance at Janina.

Again, he was entrapped by her wonderful eyes. What lovely, lovely—he peered more closely—eyes. Oh, our Lady in Heaven. No! It can't be.

He felt a sudden, terrible urge to jump through the window and run away, never to come back again.

"So you see," *Senhora* de Melo was saying, "she's been blind ever since the accident. It's been almost two years now. The doctor in Cruzeiro keeps on telling us that we'll have to see a specialist in Manaus. Maybe next year we can. But for now, we'll have to stay in Boa Fé.

"Can *O Senhor* do something for her?"

"Oh, no, no, *Senhora*," he said, emotion breaking his voice. "I can't do anything. Really I can't. I know that everyone thinks that I cured Margarida, but if I did, it was an accident. Ever since, people come to me with their . . ."

A warm hand on his arm stopped him in mid-sentence. It was Janina. "Please, your Honor, don't be so upset. We understand. Really we do.

"We didn't really believe that you could help me. It's as my aunt said; we couldn't pass up even the smallest chance."

Adão was completely befuddled. When both women smiled and thanked him for the time he had taken to see them, he could only smile weakly in return. He couldn't find his voice to utter the smallest word.

Only after they had left the prefecture and had started to walk away did Adão come out of his confusion. He quickly ran to the door and called after them, "If only I could."

Both Janina and her aunt turned and smiled at him, then left for the boat and a kinsman awaiting them in the backwater.

▼

For days thereafter, Adão was depressed. He handled well, though mechanically, all of his functions as prefect. Yet his walk was slower and demeanor more subdued, and he always seemed preoccupied. The villagers could sense that something was wrong and respectfully brought him fewer problems.

He arose early one morning, enshrouded by a cloak of dejection, and walked slowly along the path to his land. He stopped on the way at the *botequim* and bought from Moacyr Velho's wife a pack of cigarettes, lighting one as he stepped outside. This time he didn't cough. He was getting used to them again.

Midway to his destination, he spied a large, fallen log overlooking the river and stopped to sit on it awhile. There was no hurry. He took out another cigarette from the pack, but didn't light this one. He absently let it dangle from his fingers.

From across the path a fat and lazy iguana stared balefully at him. Adão had taken his favorite sunning log. From high overhead a harpy eagle soared with utmost grace through the azure sky, hunting a juicy monkey for her brood. She looked down at Adao, but decided that he was too big for her to carry off. She flew on by.

The day rushed swiftly away. Shadows darkened. Birds came by and twittered. Monkeys followed and chattered. A pig came up and grunted. Adão was oblivious to all. Lost. Far away within himself. A soul forlorn.

▼

That night, he made his much-thought-about decision. He packed his clothes and went all over town saying good-bye to his friends. He told them that he had urgent business in Manaus and might be gone for two or three months. He arranged with the *curandeiro* for him to take care of his land while he was gone. The *curandeiro* promised to make sure that everyone let their cattle graze on it in order to keep the jungle from growing back.

Moacyr Velho agreed to lend him a boat and motor which he would pick up later in Cruzeiro. And, as his last official act as prefect, he appointed *seu* Aldyr to take charge of the town in his place. Whereas Adão had reluctantly been prefect, the old policeman was elated. High position and its accompanying respect were all he had ever wanted. It didn't matter to him that he was only a temporary prefect, appointed by another temporary prefect, who was in turn appointed by yet another temporary prefect.

At daybreak the next morning, Adão left Guajará, but instead of heading for Cruzeiro do Sul, he was seen going in the opposite direction. Downstream towards Boa Fé. Surely he wasn't going all the way to Manaus in the small boat! He'd be on the river for weeks, perhaps months, if he managed to arrive safely at all.

Two weeks later, Adão again passed Guajará, this time headed in the right direction. With him were two passengers: *Senhora* de Melo and her niece, Janina.

It was nearly five months later before anyone heard news of Adão and the two women. One chilly, rainy day, *Senhora* de Melo stopped at Dona Santa's house on her way to Boa Fé.

From her it was learned that Adão had taken them to Manaus to see a doctor about Janina's blindness. While there, the women stayed with relatives on the Rua Major Gabriel, and Adão found an extra room at *seu* Jader and his family's house.

The operation was performed within a week of their arrival. It was a brief but delicate surgery. Janina's sight was restored completely and happily.

Both Janina and Adão found excuse after excuse to remain in Manaus. Soon, they were married. They had a beautiful wedding in the cathedral and left for São Paulo for their honeymoon. There they stayed, so that Adão could earn enough money to buy some cattle for their land, and a boat and motor of their own.

Janina loved the Juruá, because it was there that she was born. Adão loved the Juruá, because it had become his home, and it was there that he had found his lovely Janina. They both kept up a correspondence with the *curandeiro* who, at the end of each letter, always urged them to return soon. But, what with a new baby, a new job, another baby, new friends . . . they never did.

• • • • •

The Swamp of Dreams

Mankind has its mongers – its fishmongers, tinmongers, warmongers, hatemongers, even its lovemongers. So is it strange that animalkind has its mongers also? Along the upper reaches of the Juruá, animals who are mongers vastly outnumber folk who are mongers.

Among the mongers of animalkind are the poison-mongers. They are varied in shape, size, and color, and differ greatly in their nefarious sales strategies. There are the outspoken, persuasive kinds, such as the snakes, the hornets, the bees, the scorpions, the spiders, the centipedes, and all their many-legged relatives. Another kind of poisonmonger has a very subtle sales approach. It's a pretty little frog who lets you pick it up so that you can absorb its toxicity through your fingertips. Your payment for its wares? Your life. Of course, some poisonmongers are also bitemongers. But bitemongers in general aren't poisonous. Bitemongers number among their practitioners the jaguars and pumas, the vampire bats, the piranhas, the ants, the mosquitoes, and a horrid gnatlike creature who is called a *pium. Piuns,* like their relatives the mosquitoes, take in return for their bites a tiny bellyful of blood.

There are many others. Stingmongers (a classification which also overlaps that of the poisonmongers), scratchmongers, diseasemongers, and a long snakelike shockmonger, the electric eel.

Although these creatures may seem vicious when mongering their wares, they usually manage to get along well enough with their few human neighbors in the jungles of the Juruá. If one doesn't step on them, bother their nests and homes, sit on them, or otherwise get in their way, they are peaceable enough. In general, they move swiftly out of a human's path if approached. Among the exceptions are the mosquitoes and *piuns,*

· · · · ·

who avoid no one, animal or human. They believe with fervor, avidly, that all life is placed on Earth solely for their benefit. To them, small animals such as squirrels, bats, birds, small monkeys, and their kindred in size are their snack bars. Larger monkeys, chickens, pacas, agoutis, and dogs are their private restaurants. Humans, cattle, horses, jaguars—all the giants of the world—are their emporiums, their shopping malls.

The best way to keep from being driven mad by their swarms is to avoid their gathering places. Another good way is to learn to ignore them, although, at night, they do like to sing their whining monger songs just to keep us awake. Or so it seems.

There are other creatures who haunt the upper Juruá, but who are much less well known. They are not themselves mongers, but their fame is mongered by folks wishing to retell a myth, and who speak of shadows seen in the dark forest. There are those that are definitely acknowledged to exist by scientists, such as the *Mustela africana*, a small weasel with a stripe on its stomach, but specimens of which are very rarely seen. One of these was found somewhere back of Guajará.

Other animals have never been seen by scientists. In fact, they are hardly ever seen by anyone. One such is the *minhocão* (great earthworm), which is said to make huge burrows in the earth, felling all trees in its path as it digs its home. Some people believe that they are not worms at all, but giant glyptodons, relics of the long-ago Pleistocene epoch. Some Indian legends have it that the *minhocão* has a hard, bony shell on its back, sharp claws, and a blunt snout. One of their burrows was found in the late 1890s somewhat south of Cruzeiro do Sul in Acre. Another was said to have been found somewhere close to the Rio Ipixuna. The *minhocão* may be only a myth, but . . . perhaps?

Whether the *minhocão* exists or not, it is probably a peaceable beast. (It may be only a chimera, mongering visions of itself.) Another unknown animal that is not peaceable, one that has been reported from widely scattered localities all over the Amazon and its tributaries, is the *sucurijú gigante* (giant anaconda). It has been seen in all the major rivers, from the Amazon itself to the Xingu, the Tapajos, the Purus, the Negro, the Solimões, and the Juruá. A description by five priests who saw one about halfway between Floresta and Boa Fé, on the Juruá, went as follows: "Eyes as large as dinner plates, a body two-thirds as wide as our boat (width unknown), some eighty feet long." This is the usual description, although the length varies from seventy feet to a much more improbable one hundred and fifty feet.

The priests undoubtedly saw something, even though it was nearing dusk and the light was bad. A normal anaconda, if anacondas can be said to be normal, rarely reaches thirty feet overall, even stretched by imagination. So, again, perhaps?

Only two sightings of one strange kind of creature are detailed enough to report. All other tales of this mysterious animal are vague and undocumented. Even these particular sightings can hardly be confirmed, being second and third retellings. The interesting thing about the two incidents, being widely separated in time and space, is that the beasts' descriptions are not only similar but practically identical. Such agreement is rare, even when two different people are describing the same face from memory.

The first incident occurred near a tributary of the Rio Branco, the Mucajaí, in the territory of Rio Branco. The year has been forgotten, but it was back during the time of the rubber barons who built their large palaces and their beautiful opera house in Manaus. One of the more enterprising barons had sent a party of men up the Mucajaí to search for sources of *balata,* an inferior grade of rubber.

After completing an arduous portage around some cataracts on the river, they decided to make camp early, even though it was only three or four o'clock in the afternoon. They were set upon immediately by a large, savage creature that was about eight or nine feet tall, apparently bent on filling an empty belly at the rubber gatherers' expense. Luckily, two of the men had their shotguns at hand. They both fired at the terrible monster, hitting it in what seemed to be its chest area. This caused it to flee rapidly, out of sight among the heavy underbrush which lined the river bank.

A heavily armed search was made for the strange creature, but nothing was found.

This brief story of those long-ago events was handed down from grandfather to father to son. The animal was described thus: "It was about eight or nine feet tall, had kind of a domed, round head and a long snout, large pointed teeth (the teeth being curved slightly inwards). Its body was heavy. It had a long, very thick tail and stood on two feet as a man would. It also had two arms like a monkey or a man but of a more or less shorter length in proportion to its body."

The other sighting was less dramatic and happened hundreds of miles away, many years later. The time was December, in either 1930 or 1931. The place was near the headwaters of the Ipixuna, not far from the Peruvian border.

A hunter named Jaime Ferreira de Souza had turned into a small creek with his canoe, looking for giant river otters, which at that time were more plentiful than they are today. As he rounded a bend he saw a "horrible monster feeding on what looked to be the remains of a tapir." The monster's back was partly turned so that it couldn't see de Souza. Without further thought, he eased his canoe backwards and was swiftly out of sight. Once out in the Ipixuna, he paddled downstream three tributaries away and moved to the opposite side of the river before resuming his hunting.

His description of the animal was as follows: "It was bent over but might have been over seven feet tall if it were standing straight. It was using its front legs, or arms, to hold the tapir while it fed. I could only see it from the back but I think that it had a roundish head and maybe a long snout. I left so quickly that not all I saw registered in my mind. I do remember that it had a long, thick tail and muscular hind legs. It was standing in the water so I didn't see its feet." When asked about the skin texture and its color, he stated that it reminded him of a *jacaré* (caiman) in skin roughness and had a sort of greenish gray hue.

Only two reported sightings of such a large animal, made with a few score of years between them, hardly is proof that such beasts exist. Even the fact that both descriptions are nearly identical means little. But perhaps one should keep an open mind. It wasn't very many years ago that the okapi was discovered in the African jungles—jungles much lesser in extent than are the vast

• • • • •

Amazonian wildernesses. Okapis are taller than cows, being a kind of short-necked giraffe.

Another unknown animal has been a part of Indian legends for centuries, and has been photographed and given a tentative scientific name: *Ameranthropoides loysi.* It is a monkey which is as tall as a short man. Estimates of its height usually go from four feet to five feet three inches.

New World monkeys are generally small. The tallest, spider monkeys and howlers, rarely exceed three and a half feet. If *Ameranthropoides loysi* does exist (there are doubters because there exists only one photograph—an excellent one—and Indian and settler tales are not the same as having a live specimen, or bones and skins) and if it habitually walks on its hind feet in a manner similar to that of man, it would be startling, to say the least, to run into one while strolling through the jungle.

Around Guajará, the story is told of similar, but probably different, monkeys once seen in uncharted jungles somewhere near an immense swamp south of the Rio Ipixuna. The fact that they were seen would have become another of those memories of man of which each of us have in our souls uncounted myriads, and which vanish forever, unheralded when we die, if it had not been brought up in conversation one lazy afternoon

among the men sitting around the front steps of Moacyr's *botequim*.

The *botequim* was always the best spot in town for
loafing, when one could find time to loaf. The path
which passes in front of the tiny general store *cum* saloon, leads off through the jungle, all the way to Floresta, a good hour and a half walk downstream. Here
you can relax with your friends and have a cup of coffee,
a lemonade, sometimes a soft drink (usually a *guaraná*),
or something a bit stronger such as a vermouth or, once
in a while, a bottle of beer. For the stout-stomached
there is *cachaça* straight, or *cachaça com limão*. Quite
strong.

The path here crosses the highest point in Guajará,
overlooking the Juruá eighty feet below. This gives
everyone a view where they can watch the river and people passing by. Too, being so high, it catches all the good
winds which keep the mosquitoes and *piuns* blown
away, and keeps everybody cool on hot days.

This afternoon there were six men sitting there, engaged in the usual conversations about the weather, the
crops, the livestock. No one really cared much about
what was being said. It was such a nice day. It was just
good to be there.

Among the six men was Paulo Moraes, a hunter—a

• • • • •

hidemonger, one might say—who lived just inside of town in that part of Guajará which the natives called "The Center," but which more properly should have been named "The Outback," since it was at the farthest point from the middle of town downriver towards Floresta. Paulo was bored by the small talk being passed back and forth. He was about to arise from his seat on the top step of the *botequim,* when a chance remark caused him to stay awhile. The conversation had gone from weather to corn to bananas, and from there to monkeys. Alonzo, from Principe across the river, had mentioned a troop of monkeys who had been raiding his banana trees. Although the fact that monkeys raided crops was an everyday occurrence on the surrounding farms, it did have some slight interest for Paulo, who made his living by hunting animals for their skins. Not that monkey hides had much value. The only animals he hunted were jaguars, margays, and the other cats, and sometimes at night, the caimans, those kinfolk of crocodiles and alligators.

"Those monkeys will steal anything," Alonzo was saying.

"It's too bad that more people don't like to eat them," said Zé Maia, *seu* Bonifacio's and Dona Santa's son. "Then there wouldn't be so many of them. They'd all be hunted out."

"My mother-in-law loves to eat them," said Zé Magro (Skinny Zé). "She'll eat anything."

"They do taste good," Alonzo replied. "But they look too much like people for me to eat them."

"I'd eat one if I were hungry enough," contributed *seu* Estevão, the *curandeiro*. "But I'd feel like a cannibal."

"You know, this reminds me of a story my father once told me about a monkey he ate," said Moacyr, the *botequim* owner's son. "He had been hunting for jaguars somewhere near a swamp that drains into the Rio Ipixuna. He said that he had come down with a fever right after he had shot a monkey that was as big as a man. He said that he skinned it and was going to bring the pelt back because he could sell it for a lot of money, since no one had ever seen a monkey that big before. He said that the fever had left him so weak that he hadn't the strength to hunt for food, so he had to eat the monkey. But he did save the skin until he lost it somewhere in the swamp. He said that the fever he had was so bad that he didn't even remember how he had gotten home."

Now Paulo was really interested. Only last week old João Saad, the trader who bought his skins, had told him about a giant monkey he had heard about from some Indians who lived over on the Ituí. He could remember his exact words. "If you can find one for me,

Paulo, I'll pay you enough so that you won't have to go hunting for another two or three years. I know a scientist in Manaus who would pay anything for an animal like that."

"That's a good tale, Moacyr," Paulo said. "But monkeys don't get that big. It must have been the fever your father caught that made him see things that weren't really there."

"No. He swears that it's true. He's in the back. I'll go get him and he can tell you himself."

While Moacyr was gone in search of his father, the men began to discuss the various large monkeys they had seen. No one had seen one as large as a man except *seu* Estevão, who said that he had seen some called gorillas in the zoo in Rio de Janeiro. But that they had come from Africa, not Brazil.

Shortly, Moacyr returned with his father, whose name was also Moacyr. Moacyr Velho (Old Moacyr) he was called, in order to differentiate between the two. Moacyr Velho confirmed his son's story but stated that the monkey he had killed was not exactly the size of a man, but the size of a woman; maybe a little over five feet tall.

Paulo studied Moacyr Velho as he recounted his experience with the giant monkey some thirty years past. Although decrepit – bent double by arthritis and several other maladies, one eye lost in an accident, and the hamstring muscle of his left leg severed by a jaguar's bite—he was mentally sharp and had an excellent memory. Too, he was the most truthful person Paulo had ever known. He always understated everything he said for the sole purpose of being not guilty of exaggeration. Religious, though tolerant of the sins of others, and never preachy, he was always upset with his own wrongdoings, minor though they usually were. Paulo knew that he should believe every word he uttered.

"It was so long ago," he was saying. "But I can recollect it very well. It happened in such a terrible place that I've had nightmares about it. There's a swamp there that goes on and on. You can't find the end of it. And there's something in the water or in the fruit or mosquitoes, or something, that makes you see things that aren't there."

"Hallucinations," broke in the *curandeiro*.

"Yes. Hallucinations and nightmares," Moacyr Velho continued. "It seemed that whenever I would dream at night, then wake up, my dreams didn't stop for hours. I'd try to blank them out of my mind but they kept coming back.

"Anyway, I had a terrible fever and couldn't shake off one of those hallucinations, and I was just sitting there under a tree, when I saw this big monkey, just standing there staring at me. It stood on two feet, just like a man, and had big, big eyes. But . . . before I go on . . . I forgot to tell you that I had left the swamp. I was either on the other side of it, or on an island in its middle. I don't really know.

"Anyway, I thought at first that that monkey was another hallucination, but no matter how hard I tried, I couldn't will myself not to see it. It was real. So I shot it. My fever made me think that it was the devil, and that he had come to take me away.

"It didn't make a sound, not even when I shot it. It just fell over dead. At first I felt bad about killing it because it looked so human, but then I went crazy. I was starving and probably would have died because I had been lying around for days with the fever and hadn't the will to find anything to eat, so I skinned it and ate it. I ate it raw because I had lost my matches and my flint. But it saved my life because it gave me the strength to find my way out of there.

"The worst part, though, was that same night. I'd killed and eaten it right at dusk, and had planned to try to get home the next morning. I must have been sleeping soundly because I couldn't remember dreaming, when, all of a sudden, I woke up to a horrible screaming. It was coming from all around. Then I found myself being pelted by branches and . . . (here he looked around and saw two small girls, Fatima and Mariquinha, listening to his story) . . . by some branches and by some . . . ah, dung. It must have been some more of those monkeys because only monkeys throw their own dung at people.

"Anyway," he continued with a shudder, "I took off right then. I ran and stumbled around for hours in that cursed swamp. Luckily, the moon was bright so that I could see my way. If not, I'd have drowned or been bitten by snakes. They were everywhere.

"Finally, I reached the high jungle and loafed around for about a week eating fruits and animals that I trapped—since I'd lost my gun—until I'd recuperated. Then I came home."

"Why were you there in the first place, *seu* Moacyr?" asked Alonzo.

"I used to be like Paulo here. Stubborn. I was after a jaguar and followed it for days. I saw its tracks leading into the swamp, so I just went in after it. I'll never do that again."

Everyone was too polite to mention that, as wasted and as crippled as he was, there could be no doubt that he would never do that again.

For another hour, the men sat around talking about the monkey, and other, more mundane, subjects, until they began to drift away, one by one. Paulo stayed behind. He wanted to learn more about these large creatures.

"*Seu* Moacyr," he asked. "Can you tell me how to get to this place?"

"I knew you'd ask, Paulo," the old man replied. "You're just like I was when I was your age. Adventurous and foolhardy.

"Well, I can tell you how to get there in a general sort of way, but not exactly. You see, I was tracking a jaguar at the time, and didn't go in a straight line.

"I went pretty much directly to the west and slightly north for about four days until the jaguar veered off to the north for another two days. Then I came upon a hill, a very high hill. That jaguar had gone straight up the hill and straight down the other side through a deep ravine that led into the swamp. That ravine was almost a tunnel. The trees on both sides blotted out the light where they met overhead. I was lucky I wasn't snake-bit by the time I got out of there. It must have taken me an hour to get to the other end.

"Right there, at the opening of the tunnel, is where the swamp begins. That crafty old jaguar caught an otter and ate part of it, then it took off into the swamp and that's where I lost it."

"So then," Paulo said, "You went almost directly west, but just slightly north for four days. Then you went directly north for another two days until you came to a high hill. Is that right?"

"Yes, but this was thirty years ago. The swamp might not be there now."

"But the hill will," Paulo stated. "That can't have changed in thirty years."

"Probably not. But take my advice. Don't go. Isn't that what you're planning to do?"

"Maybe. If I'm out that way I might."

"Don't. You may not come back. Remember, too, Noemi is pregnant."

With this friendly warning in mind, Paulo left for home. It was already getting dark. *Seu* Moacyr's remark about his wife being pregnant troubled him, but . . . no, he'd think about it later, he said to himself.

As he walked thoughtfully down the darkening path, he wondered about the giant monkeys. He was sure that he could get one if they really existed. And that they really existed, he had no doubt. Moacyr Velho never lied, and the fact that some Indians had seen some, although not in the same general area, made it almost a sure thing.

There were few who knew the jungle better than Paulo. Besides being jungle-wise, he was still young (thirty-one), strong, healthy and, most of all, tenacious. He didn't look like a hunter. If he were ever to wear a suit, which he never had, he might pass for a bank clerk or perhaps an office worker. He had dark brown eyes and dark curly hair. His features were fine, almost those of a young girl, marred only by a long, pencil-line scar, which ran from his left ear to his chin. Yet, for all his almost delicate appearance, he had inherited the ruggedness and stoicism of his Portuguese forebears, who had come to the Juruá by way of Maranhão generations before. He could thrive where others could only survive.

▼

Two weeks were to pass before Paulo was ready to go after one of the giant monkeys. At home, the night before he was ready to leave, he began to gather the equipment he would need for an extended trip. He would take very few things; his shotgun, a box full of shells, his long-bladed knife, some fish hooks and line, a flashlight, some matches sealed in a waterproof tin, and some flint and steel in case he accidentally got the matches wet. That's all. Anything else would weigh him down needlessly. The jungle would provide him with his food and water and a bed for the night.

He was sitting by candlelight on the edge of his hammock, polishing his shotgun, when Noemi came in. Carefully—she was eight months pregnant—she eased into her hammock and sat facing Paulo.

"Paulo, please don't go," she said. "I have such a bad feeling that you'll never come back."

"Look . . . ," he began, exasperated because they had

been arguing all day about his leaving. Abruptly, without finishing what he was going to say, he stood up and said, half-angrily, "I'll be right back. I need some more oil for my shotgun."

In the other room, he found the oil he didn't really need. He had used it as an excuse so that he could get his thoughts together. Both he and Noemi had wanted children desperately. After seven long years and four miscarriages, it looked as if they would now have their wish. Just four more weeks. If only we didn't need the money so badly, he thought. I'll try one more time. If I can't convince her that I'll be safe, I'll stay. Now's not the time for her to be upset.

He glanced through the doorway. Noemi was still sitting in the hammock, with her face averted. Her dejection was so strong that it had become a living presence unto itself. It reached out and enveloped them both.

Seeing that she was close to tears, Paulo almost relented. Most men get used to their wives' crying, but not Paulo. Noemi hardly ever cried, so when she did, he would do anything she asked of him. After all these years, he still loved her as deeply as he had when they had first met. Now, especially, she was a part of him. She was always this way in her expectant motherhood: rosy cheeks, glowing hair, and large brown eyes, speckled with golden stars.

• • • • •

But, no. The arguments he had used were still valid. They still owed Dona Beija-flor for those three acres of hers. They needed clothes for the baby. He knew that Noemi had always wanted a short-wave radio. Too, they would need batteries for the radio.

He went back into the room and sat down again in his hammock. He turned to face her. "Noemi," he began. "We've been fighting all day about this, and we're getting nowhere."

Noemi turned to face him. Then she did what she had once before done when an argument had become too serious—she smiled; a most beautiful smile. Paulo felt an unstoppable compulsion to say, "I've decided to stay home." Noemi saw this, but said, "You're right, Paulo. And I'm right. Go, but promise me that you'll return in two weeks."

Paulo was too dumbstruck to say anything other than, "I promise."

"Then pull your hammock closer to mine and hold my hand until we go to sleep. Will you?"

"Right now," he said, putting away his shotgun. He rehooked his hammock nearer to hers and blew out the candle.

It's so good lying here and holding his wonderful hand, she thought.

• • • • •
94

It's so good lying here and holding her wonderful hand, he thought.

▼

The next morning, the morning for him to leave, Noemi made Paulo a huge breakfast of buttered *macaxeiras*, fried venison, four eggs, and half a panful of sweet corn pudding. She also packed some slices of venison and some small spotted bananas in a cloth bag for his first supper in the jungle.

Slinging his shotgun around his back by its homemade strap, he went to Noemi and kissed her softly on her lips. He whispered, "I love you. I'll be back."

"Remember your promise to return in two weeks."

"*Tá.*"

After he had gone about fifteen paces, he turned and went back and hugged her one more time. He long ago had admitted to himself, that of the two of them, she was the smartest, and he usually listened to and deferred to her opinions. But since she had become pregnant, she had seemed a bit childish.

It was a beautiful morning. The heat of the day was still lurking somewhere, waiting for the cool of dawn to move on. Children were everywhere, laughing and playing games, reluctantly ready for school. Farmers were hefting hoes and machetes for their work in the fields.

Fishermen were headed for the river with nets thrown over their shoulders. Women were carrying bundles of clothes to the creek for washing. Everything was at peace. The world was wonderfully dewy and fresh-smelling.

Guajará is not a big place. It's really quite small. But it's a friendly town, and everyone knows everyone else, and most of the inhabitants are related to one another in some way. It took Paulo an hour to reach the jungle. Actually, it is only a five-minute walk.

His nieces and nephews and godchildren passed him on their way to school. There was Chiquinha, Mariquinha, Soninha, Joãozinho, Jaime, Sandra, Fatima, Suely . . . well, an interminable roster. All asked his blessing and wanted a kiss or a hug or a pat on the head. His niece, Fatima, lingered the longest. She ran up to him and wordlessly stared into his eyes. He smiled and shook his head. She loved the jungle as much as he did, but, of course, he couldn't take her along. He embraced her and playfully gave her long hair a yank.

Then there were all the other neighbors' children who waved at him and wanted to know where he was going. Of all the adults in the village, he was their favorite. He was always bringing back some marvelous new thing from the jungle. And it wasn't everyone who had the courage to go after jaguars single-handed.

· · · · ·

There were his former playmates, all grown up now, and with families of their own. Over there, Guilherme waved. Yonder was someone too far away to recognize but who waved. Bernadete asked him to bring her a baby parrot. Adalgisa smiled and said hello. Vicente passed him and hit his arm playfully. One of his sisters, Thereza, gave him a kiss and asked him to bring her a baby monkey. Either a spider monkey or a marmoset, but definitely not a howler. A howler would roar everyone to sleep at night and roar them awake.

Naturally, Bom Jesus came running. He rubbed his back on Paulo's leg and purred. Paulo squatted and stroked his back, then picked him up and put him back down, facing the opposite direction. This was how the villagers told him that he couldn't go with them. Bom Jesus mewed reproachfully. Catching sight of Fatima, he ran after her. Maybe *she* would accompany him into the jungle.

Paulo heard his name called. Turning, he saw Father O'Malley standing in the chapel door; he was visiting Guajará for three weeks, as he did once each year. They waved to each other. He and the priest had become fast friends. They both wondered why some birds' eggs were speckled, and why some were not. Why were some butterflies blue and others yellow? They shared many hours discussing nature and posing questions about it. Sometimes one knew—sometimes the other—sometimes neither.

The older people were depressing today. From Dona Santa, "Hurry back, Paulo. Your wife will have her baby anytime now." From Dona Pipira, "Come back soon, Paulo. Remember that Noemi's only got a month to go." From *seu* Aldyr, "Don't stay too long, Paulo."

By the time he had passed the corn fields, he was feeling downcast. At the sugar cane fields, guilt was added to the dejection. At that dismal place behind the town, The Lake of the Dead, doubts were creeping slyly in. But, in sight of the beckoning green forest, eagerness pushed all those sad feelings aside. His steps quickened.

▼

There is a malady, not perhaps a sickness, but more perhaps a bewitchment. This bewitchment is visited upon some few of us who hear its sweet song, a most enchanted melody that bestirs in the human race a sleeping memory. Most never hear it. It is very old. Unimaginably ancient. This song is sung to all. In the dark recesses of our minds there is a closed door against which it flits and hovers. If only we could hear. If only we could see.

Paulo had this malady. Unbeknownst to his conscious mind, from deep within his soul, he heard this song—he had always heard it. It is a song of the ghosts of forests ancient, calling their children home. *See how beautiful we are,* they sing. *Stay among us. We are the pacas, the deer, the jaguars. We are the trees, the flowers, the birds. We are the slow, slow sloths and the green, green lichens. Stay with us. We are your home.*

Paulo heard their song. When he left Guajará that morning, he was going home.

▼

Paulo took his time, following the route Moacyr Velho had described. He had told him that he had gone several kilometers each day, but unhurriedly. Inexact but still good directions, even after thirty years.

In the high jungles, such as these were, there is no sun. There is only a green light filtered through the leaves above. To one born to this bedimmed world, finding one's direction is partly common sense. West, the direction in which Paulo was headed, was where the light is dimmest in the morning, brightest in the afternoon. Direction-finding is also partly instinctual. Even on cloudy, rainy days, those who are at home in the jungle know where they are going. How? There is no answer. No one knows how.

The food Noemi had packed for him sufficed for the first day. Thereafter, he caught fish in creeks and brooklets, and plucked fruit from trees and bushes. Fruits are usually abundant—abundant, that is, if you know which ones are edible and not poisonous. There is a saying which tells us that what fruits monkeys eat can also be eaten by humans. This is generally true. There are, however, exceptions. Many hunters have discovered this after awakening in the middle of the night with stomach cramps and spells of vomiting. But Paulo knew the difference. To him, the jungle gave freely of its bounty.

At night, among those high buttresses, like castle keeps, which the forest giants put out as roots, Paulo finds warm nests in which to sleep. First, he always scrapes away the ground litter of twigs and rotting leaves to make sure that he won't be lying atop an ants' nest or scorpion den or a snake's lair. Most uncomfortable.

Jungle nights are the blackest of nights. Only a deep cave is comparable. Or, maybe, to those who find the jungle terrifying, it is like Hades with its fires tamped out. Sometimes, but only sometimes, a moonbeam shines through the canopy high overhead; but it illumines nothing. It is only a comforting and pretty thing to see. A reminder that reality will come with morning.

For Paulo, his nights in the jungle are restful. The earth may be hard and slightly damp, but with his small pack for a pillow, and his body curled up, he is quite comfortable. Only on cold nights does he build a fire. Mostly he ignores the night sounds that come mysteriously from the darkness, and thinks about everyday matters. Sometimes he remembers chores to be done, or problems to solve. Sometimes, though, he plays games with the night sounds and tries to identify footfalls and other stealthy noises. A twig snapping softly—a deer. Twigs snapping noisily—a peccary. A slithering in the brush—a passing snake. A shrill scream from the tree-tops—a monkey grabbed by some night predator. To Paulo, these things are not frightening. When we lie awake in our safe homes on dark nights, we hear the ticking of a clock, a backfire from the street, a distant train rumbling from somewhere to somewhere. We know what they are and are usually unafraid. Paulo knows what the jungle sounds are and does not fear them.

He closed his eyes. He instantly thought of Noemi. No! If I think about her, I'll never get to sleep. The *curandeiro*. How does *seu* Estevão always know the sex of a child before it's born? Usually, Dona Pipira was midwife. *Seu* Estevão rarely examined pregnant women. How did he know that they would have a daughter? Their daughter. Noemi. No! Cattle. Their two cows. Noemi leading them to pasture. He gave up. He thought about Noemi, and didn't sleep well.

▼

Four days slightly north of west and two days north he went. It was a pleasant journey. The tall trees kept

• • • • •

the sunlight from the ground, so underbrush was small and rarely entangling. Animals could be seen everywhere if one walked slowly and was careful not to be noisy. Deer were plentiful, as were skunks, opossums, armadillos, coatis, monkeys, pacas, and agoutis. Their tracks and trails were legion. Here, a deer passed. There a puma. Here a jaguar. There some ants had stripped a branch of its leaves. Holes in trees betokened beetles and woodpeckers. Swarms of bees heralded hidden honey.

On the sixth day, just before twilight, he picked the tallest tree on the highest ground he could find, a good two-hundred feet in height. This he climbed, laboriously at first because its lower trunk was branchless, then more easily and swiftly as he reached the middle boughs and found handholds. Balancing in the topmost branches, swaying slightly in the wind, he looked out over the verdant sea of trees below him and saw, an hour's walk to the northwest, the high, forested hill that Moacyr Velho had described to him. It had to be the right one. There were no others in sight.

Although he was comfortable sleeping in the jungle far below, the waning, dull red ball of the sun which sat atop the hill in the distance was a lovely thing to watch, and he wanted to see the stars again, so he decided to sleep in the tree that night. Quickly, he set about hacking at the branches surrounding him and, within a few minutes, built an eagle's aerie for his bed. Before retiring, he scrambled halfway back down the tree, plucked a lonely bromeliad growing there, picked out the unfortunate ants drowned within, then had a welcome draught of warm, sweet water for the thirst he had worked up.

Paulo had, as a child, found treetops delightful places to visit at dawn or at dusk. There, jungle life unfolded and enfolded at its most raucous, its most cacophonous. It always seemed to Paulo that the animals were happiest at dusk, when preparing for sleep. But, whether or not they were happy, they were certainly loud. Only the eagles and hawks were silent as they sailed through the darkening sky. Their companions, the swallows, added distant twitters to the bedlam the animals made. Here in the trees, the birds, solitary and in enormous flocks, fought for roosts and, having found them, recounted excitedly to each other the events of the day just past. There were all manner of birds. There were macaws, umbrella birds, curassows, toucans, yellow-headed parrots and blue-headed parrots, tanagers, trogons, and every other kind imaginable. Even noisier were the monkeys; spider monkeys, howler monkeys, woolly monkeys, uacaris, capuchins, squirrel monkeys, and marmosets. Farther below, a margay spat, hissed, and mewed. A kinkajou and a family of coatis added their voices. Underlying all was the croaking and chirping of multitudes of small tree frogs calling for mates or announcing pompously that such and such a branch was their territory and theirs alone. All other tree frogs, beware!

Lying on his back, Paulo watched the stars come out, one by one, until the southern heavens were filled with their wondrous light. Meteors streaked and a lonely satellite moved slowly through the arcanum of twinkling lights. Bats flew jerkily past, and a nighthawk soared, chasing a fat moth.

He moved slowly and carefully in order to roll and light a cigarette. He didn't want to disturb the family of marmosets who were asleep just below his crude nest. They were his favorite animals—tiny elves of monkeys, no bigger than leaves, who fit snugly in shirt pockets.

It was a long time before he slept. The lovely stars and the peace and solitude always reminded him of Noemi. His thoughts were of her until, finally, slumber overtook him.

▼

Paulo looked up at the hill towering high above him. He estimated that it was about four hundred feet high. It was covered with trees and dense brush; a difficult climb. If he had not been curious by nature, he would have walked around its base. If the swamp was on the other side, he would find it no matter how he proceeded. But he was fascinated by the story of the tunnel formed by trees overhanging a ravine, as Moacyr Velho had described it. Of course it might not be easy to find or, after thirty years, the sides of the ravine might have caved in. There was only one way to find out.

After an arduous, sweaty, and ant-bitten climb, he reached the crest of the hill, but found that there were too many trees blocking his view of the swamp, if indeed it was still there. Another difficult climb of a tall tree gave him the answer. Far below in the distance was the largest swamp he had ever seen. Plant-filled and spotted with scattered islands of trees and mud banks, it sparkled in the morning sun from horizon to horizon to horizon. North to west to south.

Back on the ground again, he quickly found Moacyr Velho's tunnel. It still existed. Facing him, leading downhill in the direction of the swamp was what seemed to be a cave, formed, just as he had been told, by a deep ravine and by dense trees arching outwards from its highest ridges and meeting at the top, where they made a thick roof of branches and leaves. The roof overhead wasn't like that of the high jungle, where the canopy allowed a green light to filter through. Most of what light there was came from the tunnel's entrance. Paulo had to stand just inside for several minutes before his eyes became accustomed to the darkness. Instinct told him not to go this way. But curiosity told him to go ahead.

Inside, vines and creepers hung down from the trees, yet they were easily pushed aside. The footing wasn't the best. Instead of solid earth beneath his feet, he had to walk, sometimes jump, from fallen tree to fallen tree. The floor was a latticework of tree trunks and fallen limbs.

The first fifteen minutes passed quickly, but he soon came to an even denser part. Here the vines were closer together and the tree trunks he stepped on were slick with slime and bat guano and were hard to see. Taking out his flashlight, he shone it around the tunnel. His instinct had been right.

Every ten to fifteen feet, almost as if they had been purposely spaced that way, were loafing boa constrictors coiled around or hanging from tree limbs. Running back and forth along Paulo's pathway were many and assorted tarantulas and swarms of their smaller kin. Coiled and hissing directly in front of him was an angry bushmaster.

Paulo might have decided to turn back if he hadn't glimpsed light coming from the opening far ahead at the end of the tunnel. Too, shining the light back along the path he had just followed, he saw where he had passed, miraculously unbitten, several other lazing snakes. He had known that there would be snakes in this dark passageway, but not so many.

He squatted down facing the bushmaster that was blocking his way. It was his worst problem. The boa constrictors were only medium-sized. They weren't quite large enough to suffocate him if they coiled around his body – he could easily uncoil them. But, though not poisonous, they still could bite savagely. After further thought, he decided that they weren't likely to do anything. They could see him and sense with their tongues that he was too large. The tarantulas too, weren't likely to bite unless they crawled inside his clothes. But he'd have to keep an eye on them as well. Most tarantulas are only mildly venomous, but he was strongly allergic to them.

He stood up and looked around for a long pole. At that moment he felt a furry weight resting on his pants leg. It was one of the tarantulas. Gingerly he picked it up by its back and dropped it into a crevice between the logs which formed the floor. This won't do at all, he thought. Moacyr Velho never carried a flashlight. He must be the luckiest man alive, walking through something like this without being bitten. I'll have to mention this to him.

Turning back to the bushmaster, he was tempted to

unsling his shotgun; the thought of wasting his sixteen shells stopped him. There were more snakes than there were shells. He would have to fight them off with something else.

At hand was a long, one-inch-round branch. Taking out his knife from his belt, he rapidly chopped off all the side branches in order to make it more wieldy. The few leafless twigs at its end he left there.

Holding his flashlight in one hand and the pole in the other, he began to poke at the bushmaster. Since it was only eight feet away and was more than eleven feet in length, it was within striking distance. But by poking it, he hoped to knock it off the tree trunk upon which it was coiled, down onto the ground below them; or maybe he could frighten it enough to make it crawl away. If only he could get rid of this one snake. It was the only thing standing in the way of his making a quick dash past the other creatures, to freedom at the end of the tunnel.

The bushmaster was of another mind. It had gone to a lot of trouble to find this wonderfully dank and dark haven. It had only just now started to digest the fat paca that bulged so sorrowfully in its middle. Besides, until now no warm-blooded animal had ever had the audacity to challenge it. This two-legged one with a stick was no different.

Wink-swift, causing tiny butterflies to flutter in Paulo's stomach, it struck at the pole halfway down its length, snapping it into two venom-spattered parts. It was time for a longer, stouter pole.

Backing off a few feet he stepped on a tarantula, squashing it and almost slipping off the logs before he caught his balance. Next he started chopping away at another long branch, one two inches in girth, tapering at the end, and fifteen feet in length.

Again, he poked at the bushmaster. No matter how hard he poked, pried, and jabbed, he couldn't get it to do anything other than strike at the branch. He was only making it angrier. For the second time he thought of his shotgun, but remembering the bat guano that coated some of the fallen tree trunks, he was sure that that would be a mistake. The noise and vibrations would cause the bats to fly wildly back and forth in the tunnel, needlessly exciting all the snakes and whatever else was lurking around. He would have to do this as silently as possible.

Paulo killed animals only for food or for their skins, unless they were poisonous snakes. Yet even snakes, if only wounded, felt pain and suffered uselessly for hours or even days before they died. But now he had no choice. He would have to wound it to get it to move. The pole was too long for him to gather enough force for a killing blow unless he were to foolishly get closer to the deadly creature, by now enraged.

Pulling back the pole, noting with a shiver the mangled, bitten, venom-wet end, he commenced to sharpen it to a fine point with his knife.

He slowly slid the pole towards the snake, who again struck at it, and positioned it an inch away from the bulge in its belly.

Mustering all the strength he could manage in his awkward position on the slick logs, he jammed the pole completely through the bushmaster so that the other end protruded more than an inch.

This time the bushmaster went into a frenzy, striking again and again at the makeshift spear, jerking it from Paulo's hand. But it did what he had intended. It writhed off the tree trunk into the nether darkness, freeing itself of the painful stick in the process.

Glancing back over his shoulder he saw that the other snakes were still there. There wasn't really a choice. It would be best to go forward. He considered again. Should he go slowly, tree trunk by tree trunk, easing past each boa constrictor and whatever else he might encounter further on, or should he run as fast as he could, avoiding everything by sheer speed alone? He had enough confidence in his agility but he still might slip on the slick footing. If he stepped on a rotten log, a likely prospect, he could get past it on momentum. But if he did happen to fall through to the bottom of the ravine, he might meet up with twice as many snakes. He could hear them rustling below the latticework of logs.

At first he decided to go slowly. As soon as he had gotten to the third log forward, another tarantula landed on him. This one fell on him from above, landing on his head, then leaped frightened into the darkness.

Paulo had had enough. Although it had only taken a little more than five or ten minutes to deal with the bushmaster, it had seemed like hours. So far he had kept panic at bay, but it was hiding, sneering, ready to spring. The utter horror of the place would have driven many men wild with fear long before now.

Checking the shotgun's sling and the small pack on his back to make sure that they were secured, with his knife in his belt, flashlight in one hand, and the other hand free, he leapt forward.

One tree trunk. Two tree trunks. Take two at a time. Faster. Past one snake, another coiling to strike. Duck. Spider webs. Ignore them. Faster. A rotten log caving in. Jump. Safe. Another snake. The biggest boa constrictor. It's going to strike. Backhand it. Two snakes, three, tongues flicking, hissing. Duck. Another bushmaster. Step on its head. Another rotten log caving in. Jump. Made it. Walls rushing past. A tarantula between shirt and back. A sharp pain. Bitten. Ignore it. Tarantula bouncing out. Twenty feet. Daylight. Fifteen feet. Almost. A rotten log. Another rotten log. Another. Won't make it.

Disaster.

The third rotten log caving in was too much. He lost his momentum. Fortunately, the fourth log was solid. This one he grabbed and held on to; only his legs fell through the latticework. One leg dangled free, but the other jammed between a rock and a cold, shifting something, the ankle twisted. The cold, shifting thing began to move rapidly. The logs and tree trunks began to heave as if in a heavy sea. It was an anaconda, a big one.

All Paulo could do was hold on until the anaconda left. It was fleeing, frightened by the cave-in of the logs above its head and Paulo's foot striking its side.

The cold body sliding against his foot seemed to go on and on forever. Through his fear and pain, curiosity peeked out. He wished that he could see it. He heard a heavy splashing as its head struck the water of the nearby swamp. Paulo had never seen an anaconda as large as this one must be.

His attention shifted when a scorpion fell from the swaying branches onto his hand. He blew it away with a hearty puff. A fat, green spider took the scorpion's place but crawled away. He could feel the snake's body

* * * * *

becoming smaller. He was almost free. Mosquitoes and *piuns* attacked his face, but they were mere nobodies compared to everything else.

The tip of the anaconda's tail moved on, freeing him. Exhausted, he pulled himself up, ran the remaining five feet of tunnel and jumped, feet first, into the shallow, scum-covered water of the swamp of dreams.

▼

Noemi had been waiting patiently beside the door leading into Guajará's diminutive chapel. How pretty it is, she thought. Everyone had gone all out when they had built it. *Seu* Estevão had planed and beveled and sawed all the wood which had gone into its construction. *Seu* Waldir periodically gave it a fresh coat of whitewash. Zulmira, Dona Santa, and Dona Pipira kept beautiful flowers growing next to its steps. And she herself, among others, hoed the grass and weeds away in a perfect square that surrounded it on all four sides. Two tall *buriti* palms grew in front.

Most of the villagers had run down to the river after Father O'Malley had finished Mass. Two large army gunboats were inching their way past the town. They were going slowly because of the low level of the water here, at the end of the dry season.

"Noemi," a voice from the doorway said. "Why aren't you down there with the others? Do you feel ill?"

It was Father O'Malley. At forty-five years of age, he was a tall, strikingly handsome man. Though middle-aged, he was still strong, almost athletic, and forever healthy. It was for him that Noemi had been waiting.

"I feel wonderful, Father," she said. "I just wanted to ask you over for supper tonight. My sisters, Mirí and Clíde, are staying with me while Paulo's gone, and they're marvelous cooks."

"Corn pudding?" he asked.

"Plenty," she answered with a laugh.

"Then I'll be there.

"Noemi, *menina*, you're still worried about Paulo?"

"Oh, I'll always worry about Paulo, but he'll be safe. I know that he will."

"He will. As sure as the sun will rise tomorrow.

"Do you want to go see the gunboats?" he asked.

"Yes. If you'll help me. The baby's due in just two or three weeks, so I'll have to be careful."

Noemi was genuinely fond of Father O'Malley. Also, she liked to be with him because Paulo and he had become good friends.

As they walked towards the river, they were joined by Suely, Fatima, and Mariquinha, and, of course, Bom Jesus. They all made a game of helping Noemi down the embankment. The priest took one of her arms and

114

Suely took the other. Fatima and Mariquinha held the hem of her dress, and Bom Jesus scouted the way.

At the *botequim*, some of the townsfolk watched the gunboats from their high vantage point. *Seu* Estevão and Moacyr Velho talked of their days in the military. Two farmers, Virgilio de Abreu Moreira and Flávio Carvalho, tired of watching the boats and retired to the steps of the *botequim*. Spying Bom Jesus in the distance, they talked of some of his latest exploits, both real and imaginary.

It was a peaceful Sunday in Guajará, and a bit festive. The only people working were Dona Santa, who was cooking lunch, *seu* Aldyr, who was repairing his roof, and a distant woodchopper, Edison Graça, far back in the jungle.

▼

Paulo studied the vista before him. The swamp seemed passable enough. From the top of the hill, he had noticed that it reached to the horizon, which was at least a day's journey away. From his viewpoint, here at the edge of the swamp, his line of sight was more restricted. Clumps of trees and brush appeared to merge in the distance, forming illusory barriers.

He decided that he would have little swimming to do; mostly towards the middle. Piranhas didn't appear to be much of a problem, for everywhere along the edges of the water were the tracks of weasels, pacas, and otters. About two hundred yards out he could see a lone tapir placidly munching vegetation, standing shoulder-deep in watery muck. Still, being near the end of the dry season, there would be many solitary pools of water, long separated from the main body, which might harbor some starving schools of the small monsters; starving because they had long since devoured their other fishy neighbors and the weaker of their own unhappy species.

Snakes coiled on branches, and swam here and there on mysterious reptilian errands in the water. They abounded in small armies, but were in the open where they would be easier to deal with than had been their cousins in the tunnel from which he had just escaped. Most of them were harmless, and the poisonous ones could be handled with a good stick.

Spiders were also plentiful. Everywhere were silken webs, some still beaded with the old night's vanishing dew. In some places they were so numerous that they resembled solid walls, all gossamery, crazy-quilted in bunches among the denser brush. The spiders were kept energetically scrambling back and forth because of the hordes of insects which were the most plentiful of all the swamp's creatures. Moths, butterflies, wasps, bees, gnats, beetles, mosquitoes, dragonflies: crawling, flying, leaping, lying in wait.

Paulo turned away. He had already decided to wait until the next day to resume his journey. There were two good reasons for this, the main one being that it would take at least one full day to traverse the swamp. If he was caught in it by dusk, he would have to spend the night there. A most unpleasant night it would be.

Another reason for waiting was the tarantula bite he had taken. He could ignore his twisted ankle, but the area around his right shoulder blade was red and swollen and radiated pain. Unlike most people, he could expect a severe allergic reaction. Soon he would become nauseated and feverish. He needed to return to the high jungles where he could rest until he recuperated.

He had spent most of the morning climbing the hill and fleeing the horrors of the tunnel. But, actually, the high jungles were close by. All he had to do to reach them was to skirt the bottom of the hill, which he already regretted not having done in the first place. In another fifteen minutes he was back among the towering trees.

▼

The next morning at dawn, Paulo was ready to face the swamp. Except for a slight headache and a sore shoulder, he felt refreshed. He had not experienced the nausea and fever he had expected.

The day before, he had found a clear jungle stream, wherein he had taken an hour-long bath and had soaked the tarantula bite. Afterwards, he had caught and roasted on spits some fat catfish. Mostly, though, he had just sat under the trees listening to the animals in the treetops as they played and fought the day away.

During that day of rest he found the time, unwillingly, to rationalize away his promise to Noemi to return in two weeks. It was easy to do. The thought of the money that old Saad would pay him for the monkey hide, and what it could buy for Noemi, himself, and their daughter as yet unborn, quickly stilled the remorse he had felt since leaving Guajará. So with guiltless heart, he again set foot in the warm, almost inviting water.

He walked slowly at first, returning to the mouth of the tunnel so as to follow as closely as possible Moacyr Velho's route. Here, he discovered the pug marks of a mother jaguar and one cub, heading off in the direction he was to take. Having hunted jaguars all his life, he knew that unless they were terribly hungry they would usually flee the presence of a man. But a jaguar with her cub was the most dangerous animal in the jungle. She would run from nothing and attack anything that seemed to be the least bit threatening. For this reason he stopped often, listening to the swamp noises, and

• • • • •

frequently turned to look over his shoulder in case she had circled around behind him.

If it hadn't been for the fact that Moacyr Velho had told him to head due west from the tunnel, he would have tried to cross at another point. But he didn't want to miss the forest where the monkeys lived. Old Moacyr had been too beset with fevers to know for certain whether or not they resided on a large island or in the jungle at the end of the swamp.

As it turned out, following in the pawprints of the jaguars was fortunate. The mother jaguar obviously knew this swamp well. She had probably done most of her hunting here, and the path she followed was an easy one. The swamp's floor was solid, even below the water, and there was less brush. Shortly, however, he found where they had veered off to the south, leaving him to blaze his own trail.

From this point onward, everything became more difficult. Footing became mucky, grabbing at his shoes, trying to hold him back. Clouds of *piuns* attacked from all directions, peppering his skin with myriads of pinhead-sized red dots, itching mercilessly. With a long stick he cleared cobwebs from his path, suffering occasional spider bites. On muddy islands and mud flats sunned the snakes. From solitary trees, vines, and brush, hung more snakes. Each island he traversed and each brush he passed had to be cleared of the reptiles before he could continue. This he did by batting them away with his stick.

Farther on, regrettably, he had to fire his shotgun for the first time. Regrettably, because it announced with a loud roar his presence to all. An old and very large caiman, covered with algae and other varied scum, sprang from hiding underneath a pile of brush and attempted to knock Paulo to the ground with its powerful tail. Leaping straight up into the air to avoid the old crocodile's thrust—at the same time deciding that his only escape would be through the many poisonous snakes in the surrounding brush—he deftly unslung his shotgun and fired into the caiman's gap-toothed, fearsome maw almost at the same instant that his feet touched the ground. The single ball of lead, drilled with two small holes, shattered its skull, killing it instantly.

By midday he suffered a temporary setback. The fever and nausea of the tarantula's envenomed bite, which had at first bypassed him, came with full force, causing him to vomit and double over with stomach cramps. There, on a low, mossy mud flat, he fainted, frightening away its cold-blooded inhabitants with his falling body.

An hour passed before he awoke. He was roused by the hot sun, which had turned the back of his neck a dark crimson, and by a horrifying, unremembered nightmare.

As he stirred and arose to his feet, a series of splashes came from the water's edge. It was the escaping frogs, snakes and turtles, shaken from their sunbaths when they learned that Paulo's prone body was a living being and not the dead log that they had thought it was.

He swayed slightly, standing there, willing his mind to focus on what lay ahead. He felt a tingling sensation throughout his body, and his head felt weightless, as if it were a powder puff attached to his shoulders. The venom, delayed before, sped through him, speeding up his heartbeat, blurring his vision, impairing his judgment.

He had to go on. He had to stay and rest. Both alternatives were urgent, compelling, confusing. He slowly, achingly, stepped back into the water. Each step became more painful than the one preceding it, but his inborn stubbornness led him forward.

After five minutes, he came to a dark, placid pool: still and glassy, surrounded by a ring of dry muck. His eyes were almost closed by mosquito and *pium* bites on his eyelids and cheeks, making it difficult to see more than a few feet in front. Go on. Go on, he thought to himself. "Stay. Stay," came a voice; his own, aloud. Shocked awake for a few lucid moments when he realized that he was talking to himself, he took a closer look at the pool at his feet. Instinct was trying once again to rescue him. He hadn't listened when he had entered the tunnel. This time he would.

There were no snakes around this silent pool. No turtles, no frogs. A paca's tracks led into the water, but hadn't emerged. Long, white crane feathers floated in bunches on its surface. Death awaited there.

Normally, his curiosity would have sent him in search of a longer pole than the one he carried, with which to probe the bottom of this deathtrap. But those few lucid moments were enough to send him stumbling back to the mud flat where he had fainted. He'd have to spend the night here in the middle of this most cursed of vile fens.

Back at the mud flat he sat down heavily, exhausted. After sitting completely inert for thirty minutes, he washed his face, then dug from his pack some of the roasted catfish from the day before and ate it slowly. Pushing a harmless snake to one side he drank greedily of the swamp water; something he had wanted to avoid doing since Moacyr Velho thought that it might have been the cause of his hallucinations. But it was impossible to leave the swamp, and the burning, tropical sun had given him an intolerable thirst.

All during the rest of the day he sat there resting.

Often he would splash water on his face. Often, too, he would drink some of it, muddy-tasting though it was.

By twilight he felt well enough to groggily search his little island and all the others nearby for firewood. By dark, he had started a brightly burning bonfire, which would serve to keep the snakes and some insects away. Thereupon, he fell into a welcome sleep from which he awakened only once that night, fighting off some relentless pursuer in a misbegotten dream.

▼

Distant thunder, rumbling in from the foothills of faraway mountains, brought Paulo back to consciousness. It had rained softly the night before and the sky was still partly cloudy. He awoke with a clear mind, although his body ached, making him feel as if he had been badly beaten.

His vision was no longer blurred. Only two hours away at a slow walk he could see a line of trees rising from the swamp into higher and yet higher ground, sloping upwards with a gentle rise.

The water level in the swamp was at its lowest point, due to the long dry season. Its plants were for the most part sere and brittle. But the sun's appearance brought new life to dormant seeds blown onto the mud flats: dry the previous day, but now wet with the night's gentle rain. Tiny seedlings began to sprout with a movement that was almost visible. Flowers opened, and brown reeds and leaves began to green.

As if frustrated because Paulo was near to escaping, the fetid swamp seemed to try a new tactic to hold him back in order to feed its hungry denizens. Beauty. Perhaps Paulo would tarry to enjoy its beauty for one moment too long.

Pretty mushrooms and toadstools, red and rosy, white and snowy, watched over renewing carpets of grasses, hiding for the time being the omnipresent serpents. Flowers budded, opened, bloomed, attracting squadrons of bees and flights of butterflies. Hummingbirds darted from old flowers to new with curved bills, straight bills, hungry bills and long tongues—hummingbirds which were clown-colored, green, gray, iridescent, long-tailed, short-tailed.

Paulo did tarry. The swamp had discovered his not too deeply buried secret. The two-hour trek became a four-hour stroll. Stopping here to squat down and pluck a newly born bloom. Pausing there to pluck a striped lizard from a branch at whose tip swayed a lichen-covered, cobwebby hummingbird's nest, balancing perilously with its clutch of two tiny eggs in the cooling wind.

Is Paulo childlike? Yes. At times. Perhaps he's not even an adult, only a child who has grown older. But, then, is it so shameful to see the world with wonder? Should not those of us who see the world through jaded eyes, or, who venture forth into it with grief or care or worry, or with fear-ridden hearts . . . should not we listen to those long-dead souls who remind us, through their words and songs—the ghostly after-images of which haunt the dark and frightened places of our minds—that flowers and sky, forest and sea, even a bee or a swallow, cannot easily be seen from the darkness that awaits us?

Though utterly disheveled and sore of body, Paulo's mind was clear. With clarity came that insatiable curiosity which had gotten him into trouble in the tunnel full of snakes. The small pond of death began to tug at his memory. It was too devoid of life. Too different. Too large a question to leave unanswered.

Returning to that mysterious pool, he found it just as unfathomable now as it had seemed when he had almost stepped into it the day before. The rain had washed away the old tracks, but today there were more recent ones. A large snake had wandered in. An opossum had paused to drink or sniff around for dead fish. Its tracks led up to the water, then vanished. Something had reached out of the water and grabbed it so swiftly that it hadn't even turned to flee. Seeing this, he stepped back two paces.

Piranhas can become so voracious that they will eat every living creature in sight. But even they don't grab animals from dry land. To make sure that he wasn't misreading the tracks, Paulo tossed a flower onto the silent, black surface. Nothing. It floated serenely. Starving piranhas would have torn it apart instantly.

Feeling that he was wasting his time, he still had to try one more thing. He found a long tree branch and, holding it at arm's length, tried to probe the bottom. There was no bottom. A complete enigma! A perfectly round pond, too perfectly round, in fact, devoid of life because everything living which came near disappeared. Maybe a longer branch. No. It would have to wait for another day. The thought of the monkeys turned him away, back to his quest.

It may have been fortunate that he decided to leave. Shortly afterwards, the tree limb which he had left floating in the water was suddenly, inexplicably, yanked underwater. Only after being found inedible did it float slowly back to the surface.

▼

Paulo was almost there. Tall forest trees sloped upwards gently, until lost in a distant cloud bank. High jungle. Here he was at home. Here would be Moacyr Velho's giant monkeys.

• • • • •

There was only a stretch of water, a creek, separating the swamp and the jungle. Near where he stood he could see the snouts of lurking caimans among the brush which grew along the banks in this immediate area. But farther downstream was a shallower, narrower part. A decidedly better place to cross.

Leaving the disappointed caimans, Paulo walked carefully to the narrows, and found them broken up into shallow, clear-watered pools with sandy and rocky bottoms. Unhurriedly, since nighttime was far away, and with a wary eye on the caimans, he stripped off his clothes and washed away the dirt and sweat of the last two days.

The water was so refreshingly cool that he decided to spend the rest of the afternoon soaking in it. Although he had already regained his strength and sanity, a few hours of doing absolutely nothing would restore him completely.

With only a half-hour until dark, he hastily dressed again, ran to a slightly larger pool and reached in, pulling forth a fat, wriggly catfish by one of its gills. Then he ran up a sandy beach and vanished into the jungle, where he could fill his famished stomach and slumber peacefully in the welcoming arms of one of the friendly trees.

• • • • •

▼

Paulo was feeling uneasy. Two weeks had already passed. The rainy season was getting closer and so was the time for Noemi to give birth. Thoughts of Noemi were causing him to have regrets about undertaking this so far fruitless task.

Of the last two weeks, one had been spent in this unfamiliar woodland. There were no signs of the large monkeys. Nor had he experienced any of the dreams to which Moacyr Velho had been subjected. The only danger Paulo had found here was the presence of a large jaguar. It had been attracted to this area by the small jungle deer who were everywhere and overabundant. But, even though the presence of the jaguar kept him at a higher state of alertness, Paulo knew that it was keeping well-fed and would probably run away if they were to meet inadvertently.

The effects of his reaction to the tarantula's venom had long since passed, as had the strain of the arduous trek across the swamp. Paulo had even gained two or three pounds since he had been here. The high jungles, especially this one, always have enough food and water for those who find the correct balance between wariness and fear. For Paulo, it was always ready to give freely of its birds' eggs, its fruit and meat, and sometimes it was gracious and produced some delicious roots and greens

• • • • •

for variety. It always takes good care of its own, although it must be pointed out that it loves its offspring equally and might, fairly, offer Paulo to another of its children if that child were truly famished.

After spending the past week zigzagging back and forth, checking uncountable animal tracks, probing inaccessible ravines, and craning his neck to see if the monkeys were asleep or playing in trees, he began to lose hope. The jungles are so vast that he could cover only the tiniest fraction. The monkeys, like many animals, have their territories staked out and may live for years in only one area, but thirty years in one spot would be most uncommon. They must have moved on long ago.

Paulo calculated how much longer he could continue his hunt. Returning home would take less time than it had taken to get here. Now that he knew where the swamp was, he could head back in a straight line. If he didn't emerge from the jungle exactly at Guajará, he would find himself nearby. Maybe four days of travel, or at most, five. Two more days of searching was all he could allow himself.

The next day he reexamined some ground he had already covered; then, starting from the edge of the swamp, made a wide circle, sweeping much farther afield than before. At twilight he was back at the swamp, several miles south of his starting point. Again, nothing. Monkeys were everywhere, but all were small.

Paulo looked around. The fading light showed that this part of the swamp was almost identical to that downstream. Here was a sandy beach flanking one side of the narrow stream. Outward from the stream were more of the drying pools of water, more of the marshy vegetation. After the rainy season had gotten underway, the whole area would be underwater, impassable except in a sturdy canoe. If only he had more time.

Turning dejectedly back to the jungle he noticed a jumbled mass of rocks lying yet farther south. If he hurried, he could check it out before complete darkness fell. Just a few more minutes, he thought.

That's all they were. Rocks. There were some fish bones, picked brightly clean of flesh by ants and beetles. Closer to the edge of the jungle were the smashed remains of a large turtle.

A large turtle! Smashed! Only men were capable of doing that. Only men or other two-handed creatures. A jaguar might have killed it but it would have torn it apart, scattering pieces of shell in every direction, not leaving it lumped all in one spot. He'd seen large birds drop turtles from the air, smashing them on rocks to break them open, but not one this size.

Trying to suppress his growing excitement so that he

• • • • •

wouldn't be disappointed again, he ran up to the pile of crushed shell. He was right! It had been smashed and the meat had been pulled out with hands. And only moments past.

It was too dark to see anything. Looking around, he could only barely discern his surroundings. The jungle had become a dark, looming mass of bunched trees. Behind him the swamp was a black emptiness. Taking his flashlight from his pack he shone it on the ground at his feet. Scattered among the rocks in patches of sand were countless footprints. The prints of monkeys. Large ones. Almost as large as his own. He had found his quarry.

Walking more slowly along the beach he discovered more prints. They were everywhere. In one place they were mingled together around an overturned rock. In another spot they had wandered to a pool, then wandered back towards where the turtle lay. Paulo could read them as if they were printed words in the sand. There were three sets of prints. One was small. Two were large, one more so than the other. The three sets of prints had been widely separated, then had converged at the pool where they had captured the turtle, then half-carried, half-dragged it to the rocks where they had broken it open and had eaten it.

After having eaten the turtle, they had wandered, no, had run, back into the jungle. Something had frightened them. Then, Paulo knew that he had frightened them. They had run from him.

Shining the light in a slow arc among the ferns and ivy of the jungle's edge, he found them. One of them. There, staring at him with wide, scared eyes, was the biggest one. Almost as tall as he was, slender yet muscular, standing manlike on two feet.

Suddenly, as soon as the light had shone in its face, it vanished like an apparition, back among the trees.

Paulo was stunned. He wasn't afraid because obviously the monkeys had been afraid of him and he doubted that they would attack unless they were cornered or threatened. But he had had no time to react. His shotgun was still slung on his back, untouched. If only he had been more prepared. After all of these wasted days peering into every bush, into every tree, behind every log, he had truly lost hope. He realized that he had only been going through the motions of searching, believing in his heart that his quest was useless.

A quarter moon arose, dimly illuminating the swamp and jungle. The sandy beach became a silvery ribbon, leading off into the distance with graceful curves, broken here and there by shadowy heaps of rock and clumps of brush and reeds. Overhead swooped bats and nighthawks, chasing the night's insects. Frogs and toads croaked and chirruped, and from deep in the jungle a jaguar roared. Paulo sat down next to the remains of the turtle. He would have to stop and consider his next moves.

He tried to understand the monkeys. Their large, staring eyes and the fact of their being still about at dusk could only mean that they were nocturnal. He'd have to hunt for them at night if he couldn't find where they slept during the daytime. Too, he'd have to be careful around them because, even though they seemed to be harmless, he knew that all monkeys were strong for their size. These big ones were probably stronger than he was and were undoubtedly deadly when trapped.

There wasn't much he could do tonight except patrol the beach for as long as the moonlight held out. After that he would find a tall tree where he could rest until morning. When day came he'd be able to follow their tracks along the jungle floor.

Carefully, without using his flashlight, he began to walk the beach southwards, avoiding snakes and caimans by stepping around them. Fortunately, this night, most of them were elsewhere making life miserable for the swamp's other folk.

Occasionally a deer timidly came from the deep woods to take a quick sip or two of water from the creek. Paulo walked silently past them, sending them scurrying to safety, flabbergasted that they could be so lax as to allow such a frightening two-legged creature to get so near. He stopped once to right a hatchling turtle who had somehow gotten flipped wrong side up and was wildly waving its tiny legs in the air. He stopped again to watch an ocelot drink its fill, not wanting to startle it since it might scream or make too much noise when it bolted back into the brush at the jungle's rim.

The spoor of the giant monkeys was easy to follow. Although, in the dim light, he couldn't be positive, he thought that there were more than just the three who had been eating the turtle. But the monkeys themselves were nowhere to be seen. Several hours later, when the moon began to go down, he sleepily wandered back into the deep jungle, using his flashlight until he found a suitable tree which he could use for a bed.

▼

Early the next morning, after being awakened by a flock of gossiping macaws, he set off again, more determined than ever to track down his prey. He was in their territory now and should find them easily. Or so he thought. All that day he followed their prints back and forth, losing them whenever they left the ground for the trees, then finding them further on. It was like trying to chase playful ghosts who always stayed just out of sight, just beyond reach.

But he was learning their secrets. He found several

fruit trees, which he didn't recognize, where their footprints, along with those of deer, covered the ground.
None of the fruit was lying about, only hard, nutlike
pits. These were scattered around, resting where they
had been thrown. The trees themselves were small—
about thirty feet high—somehow flourishing in the
weak emerald light of the forest bottoms. They were
filled with succulent-looking red fruits, all of which dangled loosely, ready to fall and be eaten. Paulo checked
the lower limbs of the trees and could find no trace of
the monkeys. No loose hairs. No crushed leaves or broken twigs. They probably didn't bother to climb the
trees, finding enough fruit fallen to the ground to satisfy
their appetites.

There were at least seven monkeys. He came to recognize their distinctive footprints. Two of them were
small, one was medium-sized, and the rest were very
large. One of the large ones had two toes missing and
one had, sometime in the past, received a deep gash on
the bottom of its left foot. Another was bigger than all
the rest and walked with a limp, slightly dragging one
leg. Possibly there was another small one, but he wasn't
certain.

That night he walked the beach again but with no
luck. The next day he searched the forest but could find
only their trails. Either of these two methods of hunting

would soon bring his quarry to bay, but time was pressing. There was only one sure way to get one of the creatures before he had to leave.

Hungry and lacking sleep, he paused to roll a cigarette. Soon he would be unable to move and, even though he could go for days without the least desire for tobacco, he knew that tonight the urge to smoke would be irresistible. He was going to hide in ambush in one of the strange fruit trees. When game becomes too spooked or too gun-shy, there is no simpler way to hunt.

After he finished the cigarette, Paulo began to look for the best tree for his ambush. The first three he found were almost useless. Smaller monkeys and parrots had cleaned out the fruit that would have been left hanging from their branches, and on the ground lay too few that were yet edible.

The fourth tree was perfect. Fruit hung in ripe bunches ready to fall, and the ground was littered with them. Also there were monkey and deer tracks in profusion. They were bound to return tonight. Unless something unforeseen happened, he'd have one long before sunrise and would soon be on his way home.

Paulo hated to hunt this way, perched twenty feet from the earth, unable to move for what might be hours. Only the thought of what he could buy for Noemi and the baby kept him there.

· · · · ·

Time passed slowly, unbearably. With his flashlight tied to his shotgun, he sat completely immobile, already aiming downwards. A mosquito whined in circles around his ear. A colony of minute ants crossed from one branch to the other by way of his bare arm. A beetle landed in his hair looking for a mate. A drop of sweat ran down his back, tickling most unpleasantly as it fell. Hateful, hateful irritations. The inside of his thigh itched, then the bottom of his foot. A cramp in his other foot, an urge to urinate. Still. Be still. A sound. Too far away. Closer now. A deer. Another sound from stealthy paws. No. Feet. Now directly below. Munching sounds. Two animals, one a deer, the other . . .

A blinding light—Paulo's flashlight—froze the deer in midswallow. From one side, disappearing into the darkness, fled a specter, covered with russet fur, two-legged, wide-eyed, man-tall.

"*Filho da* . . ." Wait. Be quiet. There'll be another chance.

Paulo switched off the light and relaxed his finger from the warm trigger. Before settling back to wait again, he had a few moments to scratch and move his cramped foot, and brush away the beetle who was trying to build a nest in his hair, with his hair. Then, perhaps because of his discomfort and hunger and lack of sleep, his judgment faltered the least bit. Moacyr Velho had not been mistaken, nor had he lied when he spoke of this place as a swamp of dreams.

If those monkeys can eat these fruits, then I should be able to, he thought. Cautiously, knowing that he could be in error, he picked one of the juicy, runny things and took a small bite. An hour wafted by, then another. There was no ill effect. It had been delicious. From beneath the tree came utter silence. Paulo's eyelids began to droop. His head began to nod. With a start he awoke. He had to stay awake. This might be his last chance. He moistened his fingertips with saliva and rubbed his eyelids. It helped, but not for long. Chewing would keep him awake. Chewing. Those fruits. Light-headed. Something's wrong.

Without knowing how it had gotten there, he found that he had a sticky handful of the monkeys' favorite food. I can't eat these, he thought. Why is my body tingling? With a volition of its own, his hand went to his mouth. Greedily he devoured the fruit, spitting out some of the pits, swallowing others, then reached for more. His heart began to beat wildly, hammering. Bright pin-points of light hovered, swooped, then hovered anew. Slumber crouched, sprang, grabbed, merged with his body. He was asleep. Beset.

"Paulo," the voice came, deep, resonant. "Paulo. Come."

He was in a clearing. Empty of trees except for one

very large *açacú*. The ground was blanketed with soft grass. Inviting. At the foot of the tree was a small candle—lighting the forest with an unearthly golden light.

"Up here, Paulo."

He found himself climbing the *açacú* slowly, ever so slowly, reluctantly. He willed his arms and legs to stop, but they moved on. Something ancient, unspeakable, from a world that shunned and forsook forever the land of daylight, awaited above.

Suddenly, he was no longer climbing. He was already there. Sitting cross-legged, facing his fearful beckoner. It was the largest of the monkeys. The oldest. Gray tinted its sleek coat of fine hairs. Its large eyes, all-knowing, shining in the golden light, glared angrily, yet somehow sorrowfully—grief-filled, knowing of all pain.

Paulo wanted to turn. To escape. But it was as if invisible chains were wrapped tightly around his body. He could only breathe and listen, cowering as he would in the presence of God.

"Oh deadliest, most fearsome of all the creatures of the woodlands," the monkey spoke, opening its mouth to show long canines agleam with saliva. Its voice, rumbling and echoing, spoke on. "Why are we so important to you? Why do you want to kill us? Don't you know who we are?

"We are the dreambringers. Don't you understand yet

that without our dreams your heart would sleep as soundly as the rest of you? You would sleep and never awaken. Why then should you want to kill us?

"You want our skins so you can buy trinkets and baubles. Our skins! Vow that you will not harm us and I will let you return home."

Paulo sensed presences hovering out of sight behind his back, awaiting word from the gray-tinted monkey to pounce with bared fangs. A fear, cold, soul-destroying, came over him.

I'll leave. I'll leave, he tried to say, but found his throat as constricted as the rest of his body. Paralyzed. Please let me go, he begged silently.

"Why don't you answer?" the monkey asked with anger. "I will give you only one more chance."

Paulo now sensed that he could speak. The tightness was leaving his throat. But instead of fear, he began to feel shame because he had begged for his life. This led in turn to stubborn fury directed towards himself as well as towards the old monkey. Who do you think you are? he thought. I won't say one word. Do your worst.

"So, then," the dream entity roared. "Banished be!"

Paulo found himself in a cavern far below ground, chill, dimly lit. People dressed in white were moving slowly back and forth, laden with silent corpses. There was a sword in his hand. The people in white were reaching for him.

He ran wildly, seeking an escape. The men and women in white were everywhere. They were all headed in the same direction now, moving slowly down a long, interminable corridor. From side corridors others entered, joining the gruesome mainstream.

He was being pushed along with the tide. Recoiling when the cold, dangling arm of one of the dead brushed his neck, he slipped and fell on the slick floor. It was covered with soot and grease and drops of blood. He stumbled to his feet. His left arm and leg were numb from where they had touched the greasy floor. There was little sensation left in almost the whole of the left side of his body.

Hobbling, he entered a vast chamber—the awful destination of the grisly hordes. In it was a monstrous vat, as tall as the tallest jungle tree, as wide as the Juruá: black, sooty, but glowing red at its base where it was heated by unseen fires stoked from beneath the floor. Iron ladders, immeasurably tall, reached to its lip. Up these, the white-clad people slowly hauled their dead, then dumped them into the bubbling cauldron.

"God. The grease on the floor is from the bodies. From . . . Oh, God."

Could the mysterious pool of death in the swamp have some connection with this dreadful vat?

"Come, Paulo. You can't leave here," one of the terrible people whispered fetidly in his ear.

Blank eyes. Slavering mouths.

"You're here forever, Paulo," said another.

Stairs leading upwards. Where did they come from?

Some of the people turned in his direction and began to walk towards him with outstretched arms. Waving the sword frantically, he fled up the stairs.

A door. Push. Heave. Who is roaring?

Roaring.

Roaring.

Roaring.

Paulo awoke screaming.

A terrible roaring from the boughs above shook him to alertness. Howler monkeys. Daylight. Late morning.

Sanity returned slowly, shakily. His left leg and left arm were numb, having been caught beneath his body for hours. He weakly eased into a new position, waiting for the circulation in his limbs to return painfully. The dream came back to him vividly, stamped eternally into his memory.

The realization that his shotgun and flashlight were missing shocked him into complete awareness. Swiftly, half-falling, he descended the tree. Lying on the ground was his flashlight and the string with which he had tied it to the shotgun. But the gun was gone. It must have fallen from his hand while he slept, and had been purloined by one of the monkeys. Their tracks eloquently told of what had happened.

Three sets of tracks led away from the tree. They wandered from fruit tree to fruit tree. Sometimes a thin furrow appeared where they had dragged the gun's barrel along the ground. Occasionally, a wider furrow bespoke the gun's butt.

After thirty minutes of following the spoor, he found a spot where the tracks were all mixed together confusedly. Could they have been fighting over the shotgun? From there they ran, as the wider spacing between each footprint showed, vanishing completely where they had swung up into the trees.

Paulo was devastated. All these long weeks, all the privations, all for nothing. Without his shotgun he had little hope of capturing one of the creatures. He didn't need it to survive. He had fired it only once since leaving Guajará. There, too, he had another one, albeit an older, much-worn one.

He began to feel dizzy. At the base of the tree into which the monkeys had disappeared, he sat down, leaning his back on its trunk. There, he tried to sort through his thoughts.

Self-reproach. Depression.

If it had been a jaguar or anything else, he thought, I'd have gotten it long ago. I should have been able to get one of those cursed monkeys the first day, after I found their tracks. There's not many of them, but they wander everywhere. Those fruits. I should have known better.

This will get me nowhere. I'll rest here a moment . . . I'll stop thinking about it awhile. I've been trying too hard. It's so nice just sitting here doing nothing.

He watched a long line of ants file by, carrying leaves that were several times as large as their bearers. He watched a woodpecker as it darted from tree to tree, pecking holes in the bark. How wonderful, he thought. The air is so cool. The earth is so soft. How pleasant.

A beautiful cock-of-the-rock flew by. Perched on a stump. Sang. Flew aloft.

How wonderful. I could stay here forever.

A rhinoceros beetle scurried under a leaf, chased by another of its kind.

I must stay here. Stay. Tomorrow I'll leave. Maybe the next day.

A yellow butterfly landed on his knee and preened itself. Paulo felt a tender warmth towards the butterfly. A oneness.

If only I could stay right here. Right here in this one spot.

A thought tried to force its way to his attention. Hadn't Moacyr Velho mentioned something important?

• • • • •

Something I should know, he thought. Yes. He said that he sat around for days doing absolutely nothing. That's one of the effects of the fruit. That's what I am doing. I'd better get up. In a minute. Not now. I need to rest.

Leaning on this *açacú* is so wonderful. Strange. It looks familiar. It's the one in my dream. The very same one. The thought broke the overpowering laziness that had gripped him.

On his feet now, he stared up into the dense leaves. There's something dark up there midway. The platform I dreamed of. Something's moving up there. My knife. I've got my knife.

Stealthily, silently, he climbed the tree. He climbed as slowly as would a sloth. Halfway up he saw that he had misjudged the distance. The platform and monkey were closer to the top.

He climbed faster, impatiently. The platform was always a little higher. Always out of reach. At the top he broke through into the jungle's bright welkin. Sun. Clouds. Treetops. An eagle.

It was only a dream. Just an illusion. There was no monkey. No platform. Only reality. But, wait. A noise from below.

Barely recognizable through the leaves, boughs, and vines, squatting on the forest floor, picking squirming grubs from a rotting log, was the old, gray-tipped monkey. No, another illusion. But, no, it's too real. The platform in the tree was something vague. Something hard to see. Perhaps only a bunching of leaves. This is real, he thought.

Again, he took after his quarry. Again stealthily. With his long knife agleam, he descended the venerable tree.

Closer. Closer. Silence. The monkey didn't hear him. Preoccupied, it didn't look up at the lowering death coming closer.

Now!

With a thud, Paulo landed on the ground and . . . nothing. The monkey was gone. It had never been there. Yet another illusion.

No. There's the monkey staring at me from behind a bush. It can't be real. But it is real. But it can't be. I had my eyes open all the time when I jumped on it, and it just vanished. I couldn't have missed it. But still, it's right there. It's grinning. It's waving my shotgun!

Taking a step closer to the hateful creature, Paulo saw it vanish again.

There was no longer any doubt. He was seeing things that were not there. The fruit was still having an effect. But, with the absolute certainty of what was happening to him, Paulo felt true clarity of mind returning. All illusions were gone.

Reality grimly told him that the day was coming to an end, that he was hungry, that he was thirsty, and that he needed sleep. A restful kind of sleep.

Chagrined, feeling terribly foolish, he went about in pursuit of more mundane matters. Finding food was first in importance. He remembered several different fruits he had passed earlier. Quickly, he gathered some of them. They were bittersweet *pupunhas* and a fat, heavy and juicy *jaca*, out of season. After eating these, he drank of the cool water of a shallow brook, then washed his face, further clearing his mind.

Too tired to climb again, he settled among the great roots of a smiling tree where he awaited the approaching night. It was many hours before he could sleep. Fear of a recurrence of the past night's dream had him opening, reopening, and opening anew, his heavy eyelids. But slumber did come. This time, the dreams were not so vivid nor were they remembered.

▼

What was that?

Groggily, Paulo sat up. A distant explosion had shaken him awake. An explosion followed by animal screeching.

Was that thunder? he thought. No. No. No. That was my shotgun. One of the monkeys has pulled the trigger while playing with it. Or maybe it has dropped from too great a height. I remember now. It was cocked when I dropped it. It must have been pure chance that it didn't go off then.

Oh, no. Another illusion.

But what if it's not? I can't ignore it. I just might get my shotgun back. What if one of the monkeys has shot himself? People accidentally do that all the time. No. It's too much to hope for.

What direction? Where? From my left. The sandy beach at the jungle's edge. I'd better hurry.

Walking through the high jungle at night isn't difficult. Nor is it unpleasant unless one is afraid. But shapes do hover. Winged creatures disturbed by beams of light flit eerily away. Leaves and branches are ghostly. Tree trunks do seem menacing—sprouting shadowy visages, growing watching eyes. To Paulo, these things were hardly noticed. The forest was his friend.

Walking hastily but carefully, and guided by his flashlight's golden glow, he made his way towards the sound of the shot. All I can do, he thought, is retrieve my gun. It's too late to continue hunting those monkeys. There's just no more time. Maybe I'll run across a jaguar on the way home. Or I might shoot two or three large caimans. Their skins are worth enough so that this trip won't be a complete waste.

It took nearly fifteen minutes to reach the beach. The

• • • • •

shot had been deceptively clear. It had seemed much closer.

What if my gun is not there? What if it's lost in the jungle? If it is, I'll never find it.

Dawn broke at the same moment he arrived at the scene of the shot. What met him there was an incredible, almost joyous sight. Joyous yet awful, almost piteous.

Lying on its back half-in, half-out of a large backwater, its body pinned among the roots of a large fallen tree, was one of the larger of the giant monkeys, its head missing. Next to it on the sand was his deadly shotgun.

Paulo's first feelings at seeing his quarry at last within reach, and his shotgun again in his possession, were ones of elation and relief. But, inexplicably, he began to feel sorry for the mangled creature. It looked almost human in the way it lay, arms outstretched, passing from carefree life to a sudden, mysterious death.

Standing there, he recreated in his mind what must have happened. Either the dead monkey or one of the others had been playing with the gun when it had accidentally fired. The blast had torn a gaping hole in its chest. Caiman tracks and a large furrow in the sand showed where one of the beasts had dragged the body partly into the water, dragging it by its head until it wedged between the tree roots. Whereupon, by yanking with a mouth filled with sharp teeth, the caiman had pulled off the monkey's head and had swum away with only a mouthful.

With shock and horror, Paulo watched as the monkey began to move up and down, as if it were trying to lift itself from the ground. A sudden splashing and churning of the water told him what was actually happening.

Piranhas! The piranhas were devouring the part of the monkey that was lying in the water.

Swiftly, Paulo raced the few feet to the water's edge, and grabbing the body by its arm, pulled it away from the voracious little fish. So mindlessly did the piranhas feed that several of them were pulled out of the water, their teeth still biting at their escaping, bloody meal. There they were left flopping about on the sand until they either died or jumped back into the water.

What a mess, Paulo thought. The head is gone. The left side, the left leg and arm chewed to the bone by piranhas. And a fist-sized hole in the chest. But it's still salvageable. There's enough here to prove that it's truly a giant monkey. No one can doubt it when they see the size of its hide, and especially its right arm and leg. What wonderful, unbelievable luck! I'd best get busy and skin it and start across the swamp. It's early enough to make it all the way across before dark.

With his sharp knife and a practiced hand, he began his grisly chore. Although he had done this many times before, he started to feel qualms, almost guilt, at removing the pitiful hide. All Indians and some settlers ate monkeys with relish, but Paulo had always been loathe to kill them, much less eat them. They were too human. Too intelligent. Actually, if the truth were known, he was loathe to kill anything. But this was a harsh land to those who hesitated to do unpleasant things in order to survive.

There. It's almost done. As he pulled the skin neatly from the body he felt a sharp blow to the back of his neck. Someone had thrown a stick.

Three of the giant monkeys were pelting him with sticks and small pebbles. Standing fifteen or twenty feet away, the angry animals were trying to drive him from their dead sibling. They began to scream with high-pitched voices and gesture menacingly, all the while keeping their distance because of their fear of their tormentor.

With a last hard yank, Paulo finished removing the skin. Dropping it at his feet, he picked up his shotgun and quickly broke it open to remove the spent shell and to reload with a fresh one. Also, knowing well the vagaries of guns, he glanced through the barrel before reloading. A gun clogged with sand and mud would have exploded in his face. Fortunately, it was clean.

Aiming at the larger of the three monkeys, he thought,

Now I can get a good pelt. Maybe even two more if I'm fast enough.

Then, the monkeys did a strange thing. They stopped screaming and throwing things, but didn't turn to run. They stood facing him, perhaps in resignation, or perhaps they were caught in the grip of a foolish curiosity. But it was obvious that they had learned what a shotgun could do. They weren't about to attack.

Paulo hesitated. This was the first opportunity he had had to study them closely. Until now, he had only gotten brief glimpses of them as they had darted away. The one that he had just finished skinning didn't count. It was blood-covered and its head was now reposing, mangled, in the belly of a caiman.

All three were a deep russet in color. They had no tails, and stood two-legged with no intention of dropping to all fours. It was their natural, most comfortable stance. Their faces most resembled those of capuchin monkeys, but only faintly.

Why are they just standing there? he thought. They're just staring at me. Are they too terrified to move? Are they going to rush me? They look just like hairy people.

Then he knew that he couldn't kill them. They did seem too human. And they were intelligent in their way. But more than any other factor that led to his decision to spare them was the sudden realization that they were dying. The few that lived in this jungle might be all there were. He knew from their tracks that there had been seven of them. Now, with the death of the one he had skinned, there were only six. What if he killed just one more? That might be their death warrant as a living species.

Sadly, he lowered his shotgun and retrieved the torn, battered skin from the ground. With one last glimpse into their staring, unread eyes, he turned and slowly began his trek back across the swamp. As he walked away without looking back, he could hear their muted footsteps as they, too, turned away and headed back to their jungle home.

Epilogue

As he wended his way across the swamp, Paulo had second thoughts about taking at least one more of the monkeys. But, remembering how the giant river otters had been hunted until there were almost none, he decided with finality that he'd not shoot another. Presently, he came upon the mysterious circular pool of death. Next to it was another one, recently dug. Now he knew that he'd be back. The pools almost screamed to be investigated, and maybe he could see the monkeys again. Not to kill them, but just to catch a glimpse of them, maybe even to study their habits.

If only he could tell someone the whole story. But he knew that he couldn't. Other hunters would follow. Soon there would be no more giant monkeys. He'd have to lie about the location, and tell everyone that there was only one monkey. Secret it would have to remain, except . . . of course. Noemi. He could tell her. They had no secrets from one another, and she would repeat it to no one. But she couldn't come back with him to share his experience.

Father O'Malley! He'd be thrilled to come. He wouldn't tell anyone.

With this happy thought in mind, he continued his journey. And, after several days of travel, arrived home to an overjoyed Noemi and a tiny daughter named Nairí.

▼

To the neighbors and all other inquisitive folk, he did lie. He said that he had shot the monkey somewhere south of the Rio Moa, the exact spot unknown. Moacyr Velho knew the truth but said nothing. Neither did Noemi. And neither did Father O'Malley, who made plans with him to return to the swamp the following year.

Old Saad the skinmonger was true to his word. He

paid well indeed for the monkey's skin, tattered though it was. He wasn't as happy with it as he would have been with an unmarred one, but he was satisfied.

With the money old Saad paid him (a year's wages if he had been working in a factory), Paulo bought a radio for Noemi, paid old debts, bought food, clothes, and, as the old, gray-tinted monkey had called them in his dream, many trinkets and baubles.

The story of the monkey's hide didn't end there. Eventually it was carried to Manaus by old Saad. There he showed it to his wife, Maria.

Proudly, elatedly, he said, "It's our fortune. Dr. Pereira promised to pay me one million *cruzeiros* if I brought him one of these. Can you imagine? One million *cruzeiros*. Maybe I'll ask for a million and a half because of inflation."

"But," Maria answered, "look how ugly and torn it is. It's a mess."

"Condition doesn't matter. It's the only pelt of its kind in existence. Dr. Pereira is a fair man. He'll pay gladly."

Since Dr. Pereira had been called downstream to Itacoatiara and wouldn't return until morning, old Saad decided to celebrate with some of his friends. It would be his treat. He'd drink everyone under the table at their favorite club. Money meant nothing.

When he had left to gather together his friends, Maria

picked up the valuable skin and stared at it askance. What a mess, she thought. I know. I'll surprise him. I'll sew together as many of the torn places as I can. It still won't be perfect, but at least it won't be so ugly.

The next morning, she woke her husband, who was in a fragile state with a terrible hangover.

"Wake up. You told me to call you early so that you could take your monkey skin to Dr. Pereira. And I've got a surprise for you."

"Surprise?" he croaked through parched lips, befuddled, head aching to the point of bursting.

"Yes. Look," she said, holding up the skin.

"It looks different," he said, more alert now. "What happened to it?"

"I sewed some of the worst tears. Doesn't it look better?"

With shock and utter dismay, old Saad stared at the skin. No! he thought. Oh, *meu Deus*. What has she done?

"What's wrong, *Querido*?" she asked. "Is something wrong with what I did?"

She couldn't have known, he thought. Maybe it will make no difference. *Nossa Senhora*. I hope it makes no difference.

"Why don't you speak?" Maria asked worriedly. "Is your hangover that bad?"

"I'm sorry, *Querida*. My hangover is awful. But you

• • • • •

did do a wonderful job of sewing. I can barely see the stitches."

"I made them as tiny as I could. You have to look closely to see them. I'll bet Dr. Pereira will be pleased."

"He will, I'm sure," he said with a weak smile.

Puxa vida! I hope he'll be pleased, he thought, barely concealing a frown.

▼

It wasn't until later that afternoon that old Saad could get Dr. José do Prado Pereira away from his patients. Dr. Pereira, though endlessly overloaded with cases, could always find time to see a new animal specimen. Although he was a medical doctor, he also had a degree in zoology, a science which was his first love, but unfortunately was not as profitable as medicine. Yet he proudly made a name for himself with colleagues in Rio de Janeiro and São Paulo by sending them new varieties of known animals and, twice now, the skins of animals which had heretofore never been seen by scientists. He was known by all the traders and hunters of Manaus because of the money he would pay for something new, or for particularly fine specimens of beasts that were already known.

"Come in, *Senhor* Saad," he called from his open office door. "What have you brought me this time? Something good?"

"Oh, yes, Dr. Pereira. Something wonderful. Something unheard of."

"Well?"

"The skin of a giant monkey. Remember? You offered me a million *cruzeiros* for one. Well, here it is."

With his heart in his throat and with trembling hands, Dr. Pereira took the proffered skin and unrolled it.

"At last. At last. I've waited . . . What is this? Stitches? What . . . ?"

"My wife, Dr. Pereira. She didn't know."

"Of all people. You . . . Saad . . . of all people. Don't you know that I'm an expert at catching frauds? Don't you know that people—stupid, ignorant people—are always bringing me two-headed dogs, cats with three tails, monkeys with white fur that's been dyed? Don't you know that some of these things are so cleverly faked that . . . ? You fraud. Get out of my office. Take that miserable thing with you."

"But, Dr. . . . ."

"Don't ever come back."

▼

Outside it had begun to rain. It rained daily during the rainy season, sometimes heavily, thunderously, sometimes lightly, a drizzle or a mist. This was a heavy rain. Lightning flashed. The sky rumbled.

Old Saad didn't mind the rain. He hardly noticed it as he walked slowly home. In a fit of pique, which he regretted for the rest of his life because the quick-tempered Dr. Pereira looked him up the following day to apologize and to reexamine the skin, he threw it to the pavement and left it there.

Later that night a pack of mongrel dogs found it and happily tore it apart.

Daughter of the Sun

Mariquinha's life probably would have been the same whether or not Bom Jesus, Fatima's calico cat, had come by to see her on that long-ago day. But the fact that he did come by most probably did prolong the only happy days of her miserable childhood.

Zulmira, Mariquinha's mother, was at one time like most mothers: solicitous, loving, sometimes impatient, and sometimes scolding. Whenever Mariquinha, her only child, was ill, she gave her the best of care, and no matter the time of day or night, went in search of *seu* Estevão for remedies. She knew of too many children who had died from influenza, water-belly, pneumonia or some mysterious ailment, tragically irremediable.

Zulmira always took her child with her to work in their family corn fields, assigning small, happy tasks for her to do. These tasks were never laborious or even necessary. Usually Mariquinha could be found collecting the small wildflowers which grew so daintily among the tall cornstalks. While her mother hoed weeds or gathered ears of corn or filled baskets with herbs which were intercropped among the corn, she had the job of chasing away all the unwelcome visitors from the jungle who came to partake of their share of the field's bounty. These visitors were easily intimidated, even by a small child. Mostly, they were brightly feathered parrots and small monkeys. Sometimes there were iguanas and snakes. The iguanas were easy to shoo away, but the snakes were reported to her mother who would send them slithering hurriedly back to the woods by whacking at them with her hoe.

While Noemi worked in her neighboring field, planting vegetables and herbs, Mariquinha helped watch her baby. She would brush away the blood-sucking *mutucas, piuns,* and mosquitoes, and would sing to the baby—

but softly—afraid of being overheard because she knew that she couldn't sing well.

Seu Bezerra and his wife, Anna, often passed Zulmira and Mariquinha, hauling behind a cart-load of sugar cane. For them, *seu* Bezerra would hack off foot-long pieces of cane. These, mother and daughter would chew on while sitting cross-legged on the soft earth. Wonderful, sweet sugar cane.

Those long, sunny days spent in the fields were the longest lived and the fondest of Mariquinha's memories. Nearly everything she helped her mother do was pleasant. Washing clothes in the creek, or cooking for her father; everything.

At six years of age, Mariquinha was a lovely child. Her light brown hair was burned golden by the hot sun. Her complexion was, when not tanned, indeterminately somewhere between fair and olive. Her best features were her sparkling brown eyes with their dark lashes, dusted with shades of amber. Many a grown-up's heart would sadly flutter with nostalgia when favored with an innocently entrancing glance from those beautiful eyes.

Zulmira was the image of what Mariquinha would become in her later years. They were exact copies of each other except for the differences in their sizes and ages. Zulmira was tall, willowy, and radiated an almost unapproachable beauty. But she had a darkness in her mind, a darkness that grew slowly and imperceptibly over the years, changing her usual friendliness to a controlled amiability, then to barely suppressed hostility, and finally to overt bitterness towards both family and friends. And, although her beauty could never be completely hidden, she became a slattern in appearance and habits. Her hair was left uncombed for days at a time, her few dresses were neglected and became raggedy and unpatched. Worse, she became vixenish with her husband and daughter; yelling, screaming, using abusive and oftentimes obscene language. Behind her back, she was sometimes referred to as *Dona Carapanã* (Lady Mosquito).

That terrible darkness which beclouded Zulmira's thoughts and caused her irrational behavior was intermittently accompanied by incapacitating headaches, headaches which were present and unbearable at the time of her death, two decades later.

Nirceu Guimarães Jardim, Zulmira's husband, was twenty-eight, two years her senior. Everyone in Guajará called him *Dindinho* (favorite uncle). Mariquinha was the sole exception. She naturally called him *Papai*.

Dindinho was a good husband. He worked harder than most of the men of the village. With Zulmira's help, he always brought in good crops. When he went fishing, he rarely failed to bring home the largest catches. Hunting was particularly rewarding. Except for his fellow townsman, Paulo Moraes, he was able to procure more valuable pelts than anyone else.

With his money from the sale of his crops in Cruzeiro do Sul, and the money he received for his pelts, he had bought a fine, rosewood wardrobe for his wife, and a rosewood bed they had both wanted after seeing it in a shop window in Cruzeiro. Their house was no different from any of the others in town. Made from rough-hewn but sturdy lumber and thatch-roofed with palm leaves, it hardly seemed fit to contain those two pieces of hard-won finery. But even though few roofs are as watertight as those built of palm leaves, Dindinho planned to replace it with tile.

To Mariquinha, he had always been, as had once been Zulmira, loving, kind, and ready to shoulder all of her tiny problems. He was always there when she needed sympathy, a broken toy mended, or a childhood question answered.

Two things kept him from interfering with what was to occur between Mariquinha and her mother. One was his aversion to scenes of any kind. This was beneficial to his family at times since it resulted in fewer domestic arguments; or if arguments did occur, they were not prolonged beyond a few unpleasant moments. But it was harmful in that it helped him to avoid facing unpleasant truths. The second thing was something that he was completely powerless to change. He was subject to bouts of gloom. Over the years he had learned to function almost normally when he dropped into these deep depressions. He would work as usual, and smile with much effort, when a smile was warranted. Outwardly, he showed little of what was happening inside of him, but when alone he would sit on a tree stump, a creek bank, in his canoe, or wherever he was out of sight of his fellows, and stare at nothing for hours at a time, thinking thoughts of other times, and unable to rouse himself until darkness came, or until someone chanced by to break his mood. This too kept him from helping Mariquinha because, by the time he got home from his work, it was usually dark and he wasn't there to learn what Zulmira was doing to their daughter.

Mariquinha never told her father about her mother. She was loyal. Her only complaints were of illnesses, pesky insects, or of life's simpler problems.

The change in Zulmira came about slowly. It started soon after Mariquinha's sixth birthday. Her punishments were administered more often, and became harsher. From chidings and occasional mild spankings they changed to yelling and beatings; and worst of all, they were rarely merited.

From: "Watch your hand, *menina*. You'll get cut if you scrape that fish towards your body instead of away from it. Here. Let me show you." To: "You stupid idiot. You almost broke that plate. Worthless! Shameless!"

The beatings Zulmira doled out to Mariquinha were pitiless. Sometimes she beat her with her hands, sometimes with a handy stick, knobby, thorny, or smooth. The little girl never cried when she was beaten. Afterwards, when she was alone, she would sob softly, afraid of being overheard. But these were tears of sorrow, not tears of pain. Tears of the unloved.

Maybe if she had cried and screamed, word would have gotten back to her father, who would certainly have stopped the harsh punishments. But he was not to know. Actually, it was her father's example that caused Mariquinha to become so stoical. She had seen him gash open his foot with his machete when he was clearing a small patch of jungle to make room for some orange trees. Except for a lone curse word and a wince, he bore the excruciating pain as if it were the peck of a chicken or the nip of a playful puppy. He had casually removed his shirt and wrapped it around his foot, then, taking Mariquinha in his arms, had hobbled down the long path to the *curandeiro*'s house. There, without outward complaint, he endured the old man's ministrations, which consisted of cleaning the wound with alcohol, then sewing it up with a fire-purified needle and some fine fishing line.

Only twice did Zulmira castigate Mariquinha in front of her father, and both times the castigations were deserved and were the mildest of berations. The neighbors sometimes heard her screaming and yelling at Mariquinha but, though disapproving, said nothing because Mariquinha seemed to be happy. After all, she was always laughing and playing with the other children, and no one had ever seen her cry. Too, they had never heard the whacking and slapping sounds that sometimes continued unabated for as long as fifteen minutes.

By the time that Mariquinha was seven years old, Zulmira had decided that beatings and yelling were insufficient. Her daughter was becoming forgetful. This was the second time that she had forgotten to roll up her hammock and sweep her floor. She was too eager to play with her friends.

My daughter won't become a sloth, she thought. I'll have to do something. What? I'll make her stay in her room for an hour before she goes off to play. No. Two hours. No. She's too inventive. She'll find some stupid game to play all by herself.

Under the house. She doesn't like to go under there. Perfect.

• • • • •

Most of the houses in Guajará are constructed from two to four feet off the ground, and the space between the floor and the ground is rarely boarded up. This allows air to flow beneath the house, helping to cool it, and precludes the likelihood of snakes and other varmints finding an enclosed haven in which to nest or hide. Also, the smaller farm animals can use it as a retreat from the hot sun. Other houses along the Amazon and its tributaries are constructed in this manner, but mainly because of seasonal flooding, which Guajará avoids by being situated high above the river.

Although the pigs and chickens and dogs found the underside of the house a wonderfully cool resting place, Mariquinha was terrified of it. The only time she had gone under there, she had been bitten by a spider.

"But, *Mamãe*, there are spiders under there. They'll bite me."

"That doesn't matter. Besides the chickens eat them. Most of them."

"But I did roll up my hammock and sweep my room."

"You didn't do it properly. It still looks a mess. If you don't go right this minute, I'll make you stay for three hours instead of two."

"Yes, *Mamãe*."

Except for Sundays, when Dindinho was at home during the daytime, she was to spend from two to five hours under the house each day for the next year. But it wasn't such an awful place after all. That first day, Bom Jesus merrily went under there with her, helping to dispel her fear, and stayed with her until she had permission to leave. Many times thereafter, he came by to join her and to be petted. Then, too, there was their fat, vicious-looking boar, Monstro. He was sometimes there and he liked to be rubbed and petted. The chickens were always around but they were quite messy about leaving droppings here and there and weren't very tame. Sometimes their chicks wandered too near Mariquinha, who immediately grabbed them and kissed and fondled away their fears until they became sleepily content in her hands.

No. It was actually a rather nice place. When her friend, Fatima, who was the same age, found her there, she became a frequent visitor, sneakily of course. Zulmira would have become enraged if she had ever learned of Fatima's visits. Luckily, she never found out. The two children passed many delightful hours whispering and giggling, stopping only when Zulmira's footsteps were directly overhead.

"Mariquinha. Mariquinha," Fatima whispered. "Are you there? I can't see you."

"Fatima? Yes. I'm here. I'm sitting on top of Monstro."

• • • • •

"Is my cat under there?"

"Yes. He's curled up in a ball on top of Monstro's head."

Underneath the house with Mariquinha, Fatima whispered, "Oh, *menina,* aren't you afraid of that big, fat pig? He looks like he could eat you up with just one bite."

"No. He wouldn't hurt anyone. Besides, he gets enough to eat. *Papai* planted some bottom land with banana trees just for him and the other pigs and they spend hours and hours down there, gobbling up the roots. If they weren't so dumb, they'd wait for the bananas to grow. I'm sure that they would taste better than those nasty roots."

"Mariquinha, we're going to Cruzeiro tomorrow. *Papai* said that you could come with us. Can you? Please do."

"I don't know. I'll have to ask. Maybe if I clean my room good enough so that *Mamãe* will be satisfied. Can you help me?"

"Yes. We'll get it so clean that she'll have to let you go.

"Have you seen those new dolls they have at the market? They're beautiful."

"Oh, I have. They're just marvels."

Thus, Mariquinha's long hours of banishment were

• • • • •
171

shortened and made happy whenever her friend Fatima joined her. Even when she was alone she found plenty to do. At least some of the animals were always there and there were few spiders. Most of these were tiny and kept to the corners and the slight overhang of the walls which were hung with their soft webs. And were they not friends too? Didn't they snare the flies and mosquitoes which might otherwise have been pestering her?

On two occasions there were some very unpleasant snakes lurking around, but both times Bom Jesus was with her and he carried them away, probably for one of his games of hide-and-seek. On another occasion, a wayward vampire bat had come to roost under the floorboards sometime before daybreak. It should have joined its siblings in their hidden lair among the rolling hills to the west. When Monstro saw it, he gulped it down in one juicy bite. This started Mariquinha to worrying about the chicks. She had never seen him eat a live animal until now. But pigs are smarter than most people realize. Perhaps he knew better than to bother his master's poultry. After all, he must have seen what happened to the other pigs whenever the villagers had a taste for pork. Then, again, maybe he had seen what had happened to Bom Jesus when he started chasing chickens. Being smacked with brooms is painful. Of course, Mariquinha figured out, with a wisdom uncommon for one so young, they're his friends. As soon as he comes for a rest, they hop on top of him and peck away all the bugs he might have picked up from wallowing in the river-bottoms.

Studying her animals kept her busy for much of the time. Sometimes, though, it could become boring. Daydreaming helped. Daydreams of wonderful places vaguely heard about. Daydreams of becoming queen of all the animals, and especially daydreams of the sun. She loved the sun. If only she could visit it. She had been enthralled when her father had told her how important the sun was to every living creature on Earth. He told her how the plants would die if the sun went away. If the plants died, then the animals who ate the plants would die. If they died, then the animals who ate the animals who ate the plants would die. Then there would be nothing left on Earth but bare ground and the bones of what once was. "Don't worry," he had said. "The sun has always been here and always will be. It's his job to keep everybody happy and alive."

Dindinho always wondered about that innocent story. Did it play a part in what was to happen to his beloved daughter? He could never bring himself to ask her.

▼

One rainy day Zulmira was particularly moody. The rain had brought little relief from the heat of the past few days. The air was still. No wind cooled the house. Her relatives and some of the neighbors were beginning to question her about her treatment of her daughter. "Staying under the house all the time really isn't good for her," her sister Gloria had said. Dona Santa had mentioned tactfully that Mariquinha was looking slightly peaked and fragile lately. "Could she be in bad health?"

But all helpful suggestions were rebuffed with a vehement "I know what's best for my child. Take care of your own."

Last night, Dindinho had come home early. Someone had complained about Zulmira's cruelties. A scene had been averted because Zulmira was good at turning things around with half-truths. "Oh, that's just gossip. Who told you such things?"

"Two or three different people."

"Well of course it's true. But they're exaggerating. I do make Mariquinha stay under the house, but for never more than fifteen or twenty minutes. And sometimes I do get upset and yell at her, but lots of mothers yell at their children."

"But, *coração*, don't you think that staying under the house might be bad for her? There could be snakes or scorpions."

"Not when I send her under there. I check to make sure that there are none. Anyway, why is this so important? I've known other people to send their children under the house for punishment."

"Maybe you're right. It's just that I was told that she spent nearly the whole day under there. Nearly every day."

"That's not true. Listen, Dindinho. You do agree, don't you, that she should be punished when she misbehaves?"

"Yes, of course. But what does she do? I never see her do anything wrong."

"She'll never do anything wrong when you're around. It's only when I'm with her. She's really becoming a problem. She forgets to do her chores, and I know that she forgets on purpose. She breaks dishes. She's always coming home late from playing with her friends. You don't want her to grow up drinking and playing around with the boys, do you? No, you don't. She needs to be taught responsibility while she's young."

"You're right. I shouldn't have listened to them."

That was last night.

Mariquinha had been under the house now for three hours. She had become accomplished at recognizing passers-by by studying their feet. There goes Dona Pipira, she said to herself as a pair of feet splashed hurriedly down the lane in front of the house. Her toes are so crooked, she thought. That must be . . . must be . . .

Zequinho! That one there has to be *seu* Aldyr. Those old shoes of his are about to fall apart. He should go barefoot. Fatima! She's coming this way.

A friendly face appeared briefly, upside down, and a small hand waved at her. Mariquinha waved back.

The rain became heavier. No one else appeared. My sand-house. Maybe *Mamãe* will let me stay here until I finish it.

Turning back to the nearly completed sand-house she had begun to build, she deftly impressed windows into the fragile structure with a square-shaped pebble. She was proud of her handiwork. All it needed now were some long blades of grass for a make-believe roof.

I wish Fatima was here to see it. I wish I had some tiny dolls to sit in tiny chairs by its front door.

Softly she began to sing to herself. A song which she had heard sung on her Aunt Marília's radio.

Zulmira was pacing the floor. Her thoughts were those of anger. She was angry with Dindinho for questioning her about Mariquinha. She was angry with herself for having to lie to him. And those snoopy neighbors and relatives: how stupid they were. Just wait until their children grow up and become thieves and liars and worse. Just wait. . . .

What's that noise?

It's Mariquinha. Can she be hurt? My God.

* * * * *
176

Frantically putting an ear to the floor, she could barely discern the happy song coming from below. "That child!" she said aloud. "All this time. All this time. No wonder she never learns to mind. She enjoys it down there. All those phony sad looks she has on her face when she comes out. What deceit!"

"Mariquinha!" she yelled, pounding on the floor with her fists. "Mariquinha!"

"Yes, *Mamãe*?"

"Come here. Right now."

"Yes, *Mamãe*."

Dashing from beneath the house and up the short stairs, Mariquinha, thoroughly soaked by the rain, ran fearfully to her mother's room. She knew well that trouble awaited.

"You," her mother began. But her anger was too great. She couldn't find words.

Zulmira resumed pacing the floor, willing herself not to beat her daughter. A stark fear had been developing slowly in her mind. She remembered how Dindinho had casually glanced at the back of Mariquinha's legs when she had arisen from the table after supper. She remembered how he had glanced her way a second time when she had bent over to retrieve something from the floor. He was looking for signs of the beatings. What if he asks her to take off her clothes? she thought. If he really suspected me, he'd not hesitate. And naturally Mariquinha would do anything he asked. Those scars on her back. How can she misbehave all the time? Why can't she learn to mind? That miserable child. I'll show her. I'll show everybody.

"Mariquinha," she said in a low voice filled with spite. "Get in the wardrobe and close the door. Stay there until I tell you to leave. You'll not be having fun under the house anymore."

"*Mamãe*. What did I do?"

"Shut up!" she yelled. "Get in there now."

Silently, Mariquinha walked to the wardrobe and opened one of the two doors.

"No. Not your father's side. Get in my side. And don't touch my dresses. Put my shoes on the top shelf."

Obeying, Mariquinha slowly closed the door. A door into darkness. It was to become her jail, a stifling and lonely jail, for after-school hours, weekends, and the long torrid days of school vacations; whenever her father was away. It was her jail for two years.

This was a day of change for both Mariquinha and her mother. There were no more beatings for Mariquinha and her back began to heal and the scars faded. There was no longer a playground under the house where her animals and her friends, Bom Jesus and Fatima, could come to see her. There was only the ovenlike

· · · · ·

wardrobe. For Zulmira, the change was a satisfying one. The ostracism from her neighbors melted quickly away. She successfully patched up old quarrels and evinced a new cheerfulness and friendliness with everyone. She no longer yelled at Dindinho and Mariquinha. She was no longer an outcast. No more was Mariquinha seen under the house. No more was Zulmira suspected of beating her. That the small child spent an average of one-quarter of her waking hours in the wardrobe was a secret known only to mother and daughter.

Mariquinha's days began with light chores. Afterwards, she went to school and learned to read and write. When school was out she walked home with her friends. That was the best time of the day, walking home with her friends. There was always laughter and there were confidences to trade and commiserations to offer. But as her home loomed larger with each approaching step, her gaiety failed. Another part of her day was nigh: the world of the wardrobe. It was no longer punishment for wrongdoings done. It was punishment for all future wrongdoings. It was punishment for an evil in her soul which must be tamped out before it became uncontrollable. As she walked into the house she would hear no word spoken. She only saw a silent finger pointing. The wardrobe.

The last part of her day came when her father was

seen at the far end of the pathway. Then the wardrobe door would be opened, and again no word was spoken. Automatically, she went to her room on shaking legs, removed her sweaty dress, toweled herself dry, donned another dress, then ran back to her mother's room and wiped away the dampness which had pooled on the floor of her prison.

When her father walked in the door, she greeted him with a warm smile, but never with an embrace since somehow he might know by touching her that something was amiss.

She desperately kept her imprisonment a secret from her friends and her father. Once, she almost told Fatima, but was distracted by worrisome dogs playing chase, and by the approach of another friend. Once, she almost told her father, but was stopped by an inner voice which bespoke violence to her mother.

She kept her secret, and her mother's, not out of fear of what her mother would do in retaliation, but because of her indestructible loyalty. Her mother loved her, did she not? Perhaps she really did deserve her punishment. Or maybe something was wrong with her mother, not her, not herself. Sometimes glimmerings in her mind told her that she could not endure the wardrobe. Sometimes they hinted that she'd die there, and that she must

• • • • •

escape. But none of these glimmerings of thought formed themselves into words. They were fleet: passing in and out of her mind, darting from dark corners to dark burrows.

Towards her tenth birthday, she began to become moody. One day she would be cheerful, sorrowful the next. Dindinho began to worry that his daughter had inherited his feelings of deep melancholy. Neither Mariquinha nor anyone else had ever known about his problem. Yet she was doing the same things that he did. She would sit for hours staring out of the window, daydreaming as the world passed unnoticed. She would sit in her room watching the walls, filled with pangs of yearning for unknown things, things of which she knew nothing, and to which she could give no name, yearnings which brought hidden tears. But when people began to question her she quickly learned to do as her father had done before her. She smiled and awoke to reality. Yet, when alone again, sorrow and yearning would return with new intensity.

There were two things to occupy her mind during her imprisonments. There were the voices. The voices of her mother conversing animatedly with visitors who were never aware of her silent presence. Conversations of new dresses, crops, cooking, and of more worldly matters. Then there were her fancies and daydreams. Daydreams which became more real with each dark hour of confinement.

Her daydreams began to blend with the brilliant shaft of light which came from the keyhole. It gradually became the focus of all of her reveries until it became her friend and solace. Every day she came to her new world. Each day was exactly like the one just passed. As the door closed behind her, the heat grew so intense that her sweat formed beadlets, then droplets, then rivulets: rivulets which felt like itchy, crawling bugs as they crept over her body. She was joined by six companions. Their names were heat, sweat, cramps, darkness, thirst, and the shaft of light. The first five were cruel torturers. The shaft of light was kind and benevolent. It was, at first, her link to the world. It became, at last, her only world— the sun. To his golden self, she gave her golden self, her thoughts, her hopes, her songs, her poems, and her love. He took all of these things in his powerful hands and disentangled the despair there enmeshed and cast it to his radiant hounds. He took her hand in his and led her far away, from a land of hurt to a land of stillness and sweetness.

At school. Classes.

At school she thought of the sun. When her teacher taught her pupils about the old kings of Brazil, she translated what she heard into an imperial sun with all the glorious trappings of an otherworld empire. Dom Pedro II became *Dom Sol do Ceu* (Lord Sun of the Sky). Could there be princes and princesses? Oh, yes, of course. And they must each have a beautiful castle. And if there are princes and princesses then there must be a queen.

"Mariquinha!" her teacher (who was also her Aunt Gloria) would say. "Pay attention. Stop looking out of the window."

Mass. Father O'Malley.

Would Father O'Malley visit the sun once a month just as he comes to visit us? Would there be a tiny chapel like ours? No, surely not. It would be a cathedral. It would be filled with people.

"Mariquinha!" her mother would whisper. "Make the sign of the cross. Pay attention."

The marketplace in Cruzeiro do Sul with her father.

"*Papai?* What kind of fish is this?"

"This one is a *tambaquí*. It's a big one. That one there is a *jaraquí*. And those are *mandins*. But you know what *mandins* are. We eat enough of them."

I'll have rivers on the sun, she thought. They'll be just like the Juruá, except that they won't be scary and dark. You'll be able to see the bottom and there'll only be nice fish. There won't be any piranhas or electric eels or *candirús*. I'll be able to swim in the rivers and maybe I'll have a dolphin to play with. What can I name him?

"Mariquinha, do you feel all right? Why are you staring at that *tambaquí*?"

"*Papai?* Why does it hurt to stare at the sun?"

"The sun? Well, because it's so bright. Don't ever stare at it. It could make you go blind."

Her hammock.

At night in her hammock the sun broke into her sleep with pleasant callings. In her night-dreams, though, she had little control over the directions in which her thoughts turned. She would soar through the fiery but incongruously cool air and inspect her domains far below. She would dance at masked balls, swim with her dolphin in deep rivers, converse with bewhiskered *mandins*. Fatima and Bom Jesus were always there. So were her mother and father and all her relatives. It was a clear, bright world. A real world. But sometimes, with terrible malice, one of her dreamfolk would turn on her. It was always the same one. The queen. Sometimes the queen would smile at her, a beautiful smile of love. Whenever she did this, Mariquinha's slumbering body would bestir itself. Her heart would beat swiftly. Soft moans of joy would come from her hammock, and tears would dampen her cheeks. But often, the queen would chase her from her castles with outstretched arms and taloned hands. Hands of spite and hatred. At this point she would awaken to a black night and curl in upon herself with fear.

▼

A Thursday came. Dindinho had left before dawn in a canoe laden with chickens and pigs for the market in Cruzeiro. He would be gone until nightfall. Tomorrow was Mariquinha's tenth birthday. There was that bed he had always wanted her to have, and Zulmira wanted some cloth so that she could make a new dress for her daughter.

It had started early that morning. Zulmira's head was aching as it had begun to do more often of late. Mariquinha hadn't heard her when she had called from the other room.

"Mariquinha. Are you deaf? Are you loafing in your room again? I've called you three times."

"I'm sorry, *Mamãe*. I didn't hear you."

"Run down to the well and bring some water. Now."

"Yes, *Mamãe*."

Ten minutes later, Mariquinha was back with the water. Without another word, Zulmira pointed towards the wardrobe. Only an hour today, she thought. Tomorrow's her birthday.

Mariquinha returned to her cubbyhole. She had now begun to think of the wardrobe as a house. It had hems of dresses for a roof, four wooden walls, a hard, wooden floor, and a window, the keyhole, which overlooked a land from which she was forever estranged.

She sat staring at the keyhole. If she craned her neck, she could see through it into the room. But, no. It wasn't a keyhole. It was her shining friend.

The sweat began. Following closely came the thirst. Yet to come, but coming with certainty, jaunty and gloating, was the pain of the cramps.

"Marília. Come in, *menina*," Zulmira said. "What brings you this way?"

"I need to see the *curandeiro* for some hookworm medicine for Marco. He's starting to lose weight again. If you have nothing to do, will you come with me? I hate to walk through those woods by myself. It's too swampy."

"I'd love to. Would you like some coffee before we go?"

"Yes, thank you."

From the wardrobe, a thought. The queen will like me if I make her a dress. Maybe *Mamãe* can show me how to sew. I wonder. Would she like a pink dress?

From the room, a question. "Did you hear about Sergio and Valentina?"

"No. What happened?"

The voices droned. They were as the chatter of par-

· · · · ·

rots. The keyhole became brighter, and Mariquinha's dreams became fixed upon her golden castles. Her thoughts were of golden promenades, balustrades, colonnades, and amber gardens with yellow and crimson flowers, above which darted green and blue humming-birds seeking sugary nectar. The water was not golden. It showered forth silver from marble fountains whenever she passed by, just in case she was thirsty.

"Your coffee is wonderful. You must have roasted it this morning."

"Yes. An hour ago."

Two sets of footsteps leaving. One returning.

"Mariquinha. You can come out. Sweep the house, then you can go play with your friends. I'm going with Aunt Marília to see the *curandeiro,* and I'll be back by lunch. Be sure and be here."

Mariquinha was lost in her thoughts. A garden of my own! Why didn't I think of that before? My own flowers. What can I have? Roses! Beautiful red roses. And no thorns. I could lie among them and not get scratched, and they wouldn't get mashed.

It was 8:30 A.M.

At noon, footsteps again sounded across the floorboards. "Mariquinha! Mariquinha!"

More footsteps. Angry ones.

"Where is that girl? She's never done this before.

This is deliberate. That broom hasn't been touched and she's still out playing. Defiant, stupid, idiot girl. Birthday or not, she'll pay for this."

If there had been a door to slam, Zulmira would have slammed it as she left the house to search the village for her daughter.

Heat. Intolerable heat. Thirst. Unquenchable thirst. Sweat. Salty sweat. A canopy of dress bottoms, dark walls, and a tiny sun.

Why can't I see the Sun Lord's face? Would I be blinded if I looked directly at him? Does he have a beard? I know he must be handsome. I love his long, white robe. I love him. I know he loves me. I wish I could really go there.

2:00 P.M.

"I've looked everywhere, Dona Santa. None of the children have seen her. I'm getting worried."

"Have you seen all the children?"

"No. There's too many."

"Well then, she probably went off with some of the ones you haven't talked to. Come on in and have some corn pudding. I just took it from the fire."

Somewhere in the jungle, a wasp built a paper house. Somewhere in the river, a fish splashed. Somewhere in the blue sky, a bird sang to her mate.

My garden is so nice. I love being here. Oh, no. A bug has been chewing on this rose. And there! It chewed on that one too. I'll just have to sic Bom Jesus on him. Where is that cat? Oh, I forgot. He and Fatima are in the palace taking a nap. I won't disturb him now. I think I'll take a nap too.

Those rainbows are just lovely. I'm not at all sleepy. I think I'll climb one before I take a nap.

4:30 P.M.

"I shouldn't have stayed so long, Dona Santa. But it's always so nice to sit here and talk, and forget about chores for a while."

"Zulmira, if you don't find Mariquinha, come get me and I'll help you look for her. But I'm sure that she'll be home when you get there."

Zulmira found the schoolhouse deserted. She questioned Moacyr Velho, then walked to the bluff in front of the *botequim* and looked up and down the river.

Thank you, Bom Jesus. You're the best cat in the whole world. Those bugs won't be back. Good morning, Dom Sol.

Good morning, Mariquinha. What a beautiful garden you have. Did you grow those roses all by yourself?

Mostly. Fatima and Bom Jesus helped me plant them.

You're such an intelligent girl, Mariquinha. Will you plant a garden for me, too?

Yes. Of course. And I'll have Bom Jesus chase away the bugs.

Dom Sol? Why can't I see your face?

If you saw my face, it would hurt your eyes terribly. I can't let that happen to you. I love you, you know.

Yes. I know. I love you too. So much. Dom Sol? Will you always shine so that everything on Earth will stay alive? You won't leave us, will you?

5:30 P.M.

"Where can she be, Dona Santa? Could she have gone down to the river by herself? God! She could have fallen in and drowned."

"We'll find her. She'll be safe. Why don't you check the schoolhouse again? I'll see if she's gone to see old Sebastião."

Clouds passed swiftly overhead in the late afternoon sky, obscuring, then uncovering the waning sun. Busy mortals hardly noticed as the Earth brightened, then darkened, then brightened again. After all, of what possible import could it be?

Mariquinha's keyhole sun flickered. Dark, then light.

Dom Sol! What is wrong? Please don't go away.

I feel so weak, Mariquinha. I must have worked too hard. I have to leave.

No. Oh please stay.

So long.

Will you be back? Dom Sol. Will you be back? Where are you? It's getting dark!

Almost dusk.

The sounds of weeping.

"Mariquinha. Is that you?"

Zulmira rushed into her room and opened the wardrobe door.

"Oh, *filhinha*. What have I done? Didn't you hear me tell you to leave? *Queridinha*. I won't ever punish you again."

"*Mamãe*, my legs won't move. Why is the room so dark?"

Zulmira picked up her daughter's sodden and cramped body and deposited her on the bed.

"*Filhinha, filhinha*. Mariquinha. I'm just so sorry. Wait here. I'll run get you some water."

Zulmira sped from the room, then returned with a large glass of water which Mariquinha greedily gulped down.

Mariquinha sat up and stared through the window. With panic in her voice, she asked her mother, "Where is the sun? He's going away. We'll all die, and I'll never see him again."

"You're feverish, *minha filha*. It's just getting close to sundown. Lie back down and I'll get some more water."

"*Mamãe*. I must bring him back."

Saying this, the fearful child ran past her mother, eluding her grasp. Before Zulmira could react, Mariquinha was out the doorway, running towards the western abode of the setting sun.

The unknowable, incomprehensible yearning which

• • • • •

had begun to govern her life flew through her as Mariquinha raced from the house, through the corn fields, past the swampy lake at the fields' end.

Following behind her daughter, barely able to keep her within sight, was Zulmira. She called, called, and called again. But Mariquinha was heedless.

"Mariquinha! Where are you going? Mariquinha! Stop!"

Each in turn passed Paulo and Noemi's house.

"Paulo," his wife called from the kitchen. "Did you see that?"

"See what?"

"Zulmira is chasing Mariquinha into the jungle, yelling for her to stop."

At Noemi's side now, Paulo said, "Strange. I wonder what's wrong?"

"It's almost dark, Paulo. Go after them. They'll get lost."

"Was Dindinho with them?"

"No. I think he went to Cruzeiro."

"I'll get my flashlight."

Within seconds, Paulo had joined the chase. Zulmira and Mariquinha were by now out of sight, but he could follow them by the sounds they made crashing through the undergrowth.

Zulmira could see only a darting patch of white far

ahead. They were now on a jungle path, seldom used, difficult to follow. Above the forest, the sun could still be seen at the horizon, but here below the canopy, shadows were merging into early night. Branches clutched and animals scurried.

Mariquinha wasn't fleeing aimlessly. She had a goal, the *Colina das Bruxas* (Witches' Hill). The hill was a low one, townside. The other side fell into a narrow valley. From its summit, the trackless jungles to the west could be seen. It was called Witches' Hill because it was bare of all vegetation except for a soft covering of green grass, a fact inexplicable since the jungle otherwise dominated all land not constantly tilled or grazed. Perhaps, said some, this was a haunt of the devil's spawn.

Mariquinha ran to the top of the hill and faced half a sun. The other half was already below the trees. At the same moment, Zulmira broke from the jungle at the bottom of the hill. A pace behind was Paulo who, fleeter of foot, had caught up.

Something, something never understood, held the two adults back. Probably, it was the utter beauty and unearthly strangeness of what they beheld. The hill and the glade below were aglow with the last flaring red fires of the fading sun. Each leaf, each blade of grass was scintillating, alive with luminescence. Facing Mariquinha, perched on a dead limb, were two silky anteaters, bowing ever so slowly in her direction. This, for reasons of their own, is something that the little creatures often do. But now it seemed as if they were in the presence of their princess and were bestowing homage.

Mariquinha, her body haloed and shimmering with ethereal flames, raised her arms high above her head and sang—sang with a voice that in its lovely sorrowfulness could only have been woven from the silken strands of lost souls, taught by fairy princes and princesses in the wonderful golden castles of the dying sun. Only a daughter of the sun could so enchant the Earth with a song so beautiful that everyone who heard thrilled with the same sadness and yearning.

Oh, such a song she sang! The precise words have been forgotten, but the wonderful melody of Mariquinha's song yet lingers in the memories of the people of Guajará. Whenever Dindinho is known to be out of town, someone, somewhere, will find words of their own. It might be a woman working in the fields, or one washing clothes in the creek, or it might be a schoolgirl who will sing it softly to herself as she does her morning or evening chores. It is a woman's song. No man could ever sing it so well. But they too remember. It always echoes in their minds whenever the sun makes itself known by rising or setting or warming their backs.

She sang to her Father, Dom Sol, a song of praise, a

• • • • •

song of lament, a song crying for him not to leave her, to take her with him, to become one with her. She sang of his blue sky, of his green grasses, of his warm folk in the wide world. She sang of his trees that grow, of his flowers that bloom, of his folk that dance in the wide world. She sang of his falling rain, of his roving clouds, of his singing folk in the wide world. Oh, blessed be, Father Sun, she sang. Do not leave your daughter bereft.

And then Mariquinha's beautiful paean stopped. As if to say farewell, the sun sent forth a solitary bright flash, then vanished below the jungle, leaving the world with night and the evening star.

Mariquinha fell to the ground, broken, betrayed, and sobbing with heartbreak. Knowing of the finality of earthly love and of her place in the sun; lost forever.

▼

On that fateful night—the night which ended Mariquinha's imprisonment in the inferno of the wardrobe—all households, all paths being trodden, all boats being docked, all fell silent. Conversations halted, arguments were forgotten. Of all those who heard Mariquinha sing, only the babies were unmoved. Those being suckled, suckled on.

When Paulo, Zulmira, and Mariquinha were spotted coming back from the jungle, those of the village who lived nearby gathered around. They gathered because of curiosity, but also from a desire to help, if help was needed. Mariquinha was Dindinho and Zulmira's child, but all the children belonged to everyone and were watched after by all.

Rushing from Mariquinha's house were Dona Santa, Dindinho, who had returned only thirty minutes before from Cruzeiro do Sul with his daughter's new bed, and Noemi, who had hurried to advise them of what had happened.

That something momentous had occurred was evident. Paulo was carrying a weeping, heartbroken Mariquinha in his arms. Following closely behind, holding on to Paulo's shirt with one hand and shakily lighting their way with the flashlight in her other hand, was Zulmira, also weeping, fighting back hysteria.

Recovering from his shock, Dindinho ran to Paulo and gently took Mariquinha from his arms and carried her into the house. Dona Santa and Noemi tried to soothe Zulmira, who began to wail and call for her daughter. It was some time before all the commotion had abated.

After all was quiet, five of the remaining six adults sat around a dim candle in Zulmira's kitchen. Zulmira and Mariquinha were both fast asleep. The *curandeiro* had given them a sedative, hastily brewed from roots and

• • • • •

herbs. The five were *seu* Aldyr, the policeman; *seu* Jader, the temporary prefect; *seu* Estevão, the *curandeiro*; Dindinho; and Dona Santa. Answers had to be found, and a course of action had to be plotted.

The prefect, his face sharpened by the harsh candle-shadows, was the first to speak. As always, he was immaculate. His shiny black hair was groomed to perfection, his clothes were freshly cleaned and ironed, and his shoes were polished to a lustrous brown, although soiled by cow manure he had stepped in when leaving the prefecture.

"I've only been back for a few months, and I don't know everyone well enough to understand everything that happens here. This child I've seen only in passing, but even though I'm ignorant of the true situation, I'm beginning to think that this whole thing is overblown. After all, mothers do sometimes chase daughters, and sometimes daughters do run from mothers. I'll admit, though, that I've never heard such a sweet voice as this girl has." Here he chuckled shamefacedly. "I thought for a moment that I was hearing an angel. Does she always sing so beautifully?" he asked of no one in particular.

"*Não, Senhor,*" Dona Santa replied. "I've never heard her sing."

"Sometimes she does sing to herself," Dindinho said. "But she's always been too timid to sing loudly enough for others to hear."

"Did you hear those words?" *seu* Aldyr ventured. "Those were witches' words. Those were . . ."

The policeman's sentence was left unfinished. Dindinho had grabbed him by the collar and had begun to shake him violently.

"Look here, Aldyr! My daughter is not a witch. I won't have anyone saying such things."

"Please, Dindinho," sputtered *seu* Aldyr, who normally would have become enraged at being manhandled. "You're distraught. I didn't mean that Mariquinha is a witch. You know that I love her almost as much as you do."

"Yes, I know," Dindinho said. "I'm sorry. I shouldn't have done that."

"What I really meant to say," *seu* Aldyr continued, after an embarrassed silence, "was that maybe someone influenced her to run off into the jungle and sing that song. No one knows where she's been all day. Dona Santa and Zulmira searched everywhere for her."

"Listen to me," *seu* Jader interrupted. "I won't have anyone speak of witchcraft, or"—here, he looked meaningfully at the *curandeiro*—"spirit possession."

Speaking pointedly to the old man, he said, "I know

• • • • •
198

all about what happened to Margarida, *seu* Estevão. I haven't done anything about it because the man I left in charge during my absence, Adão, asked me not to. But I will not condone one more séance or one more exorcism in my prefecture. I will not put up with superstitions.

"However," he added, softening his criticism, "you have been doing a good job with your homemade remedies. I've seen the results of them tonight. So, maybe I'll let you continue until we can get a doctor to come here to stay. But as I said before, witchcraft and such things are out."

Taken aback by this attack, the *curandeiro* momentarily could think of no reply. Then, in a voice shaky with emotion, he answered, "Mariquinha isn't possessed. I think I know what is wrong with her, but before I give an opinion, I'd like to ask some questions."

After a pause in which no one responded, he continued. "You are correct, your Honor, in saying that daughters have been known to run from their mothers. But I know Mariquinha. She would never run from Zulmira. She was running to something. Not from something. And I, too, thought I heard an angel. Maybe, in a sense, she was an angel. She seemed to be a voice from another world. Please. Before you interrupt. I didn't mean that superstitiously.

• • • • •

199

"Dona Santa," he said. "I could find no sign of fever. Could you?"

"No, *seu* Estevão. Except for feeling clammy from sweat or water, she seemed all right."

"It was sweat," he stated. "She was badly dehydrated. I gave her two full glasses of water and she drank both of them, and wanted more.

"Well, my next question. Did Zulmira tell you that she knew nothing?"

"Yes, and I believe her. She said that when she came home, she found Mariquinha in her room, and, before she could ask her where she had been, the poor thing ran from the house calling for the sun. Poor, poor child."

"Does Mariquinha still insist that the sun has gone away forever?"

"I think that I made her see that the sun was only setting and that it'd be back tomorrow. But she still wanted to wait up and see for herself. That medicine you gave her put her right to sleep, though."

"You did check to see whether or not she had been injured?"

"Yes. I could find no signs. And she mentioned nothing about being hurt."

"I just wish I knew where she has been all day," the *curandeiro* said. "Wouldn't she tell you anything at all?"

"She said that she had been home all day, but we

know that that isn't true. Zulmira came back to the house four or five times looking for her."

"Maybe we'll never know," he said wistfully.

"Dindinho?" he asked the troubled father. "Lately, has she been behaving differently?"

"Yes. I've been thinking about that. She's seemed depressed, and Zulmira has told me that she stays in her room sometimes just staring at nothing."

"Yes," Dona Santa added. "Gloria tells me that she daydreams during classes. She used to be an attentive student."

"The strange thing," the *curandeiro* said, as if he were talking to himself, "is that song. That melody was utterly beautiful. But I've never heard it before. No one has. Did she invent it herself? And those words. They were coherent. Could a ten-year-old child make up such strange words just on the moment? Mariquinha is very intelligent. But, even so . . ."

He continued. "There is one thing that I noticed. She is becoming evasive. At first, she told me how the sun had gone away and left her behind; then, when she saw that I didn't believe her, she tried to change the subject. I hope so much that she doesn't try to hide what's bothering her. If she does, we'll be unable to help."

"She's not crazy, *seu* Estevão," Dindinho stated, hopelessly.

"No. She's not. But . . ."

• • • • •
201

"But, what?"

"I think that she has had a nervous breakdown."

"That makes sense, *seu* Estevão," the prefect said. Reluctantly, he was beginning to respect the old man. "But does this happen to children so young? Are you sure?"

"No. I'm not positive. But Father O'Malley will be here tomorrow. He's had some training. We'll ask him. He'll be busy hearing confessions and preparing for Sunday's Mass, but I know that he'll find time to see her. In the meantime, Dindinho, keep a sharp eye on her. She should sleep all night, but don't take any chances."

"Why don't you stay here tonight, *seu* Estevão?" Dindinho asked. "Would you mind? I'll set up Mariquinha's new bed. You can sleep in it."

"Well, all right. It's a long walk home. Maybe I can help during the night."

It was decided. They would consult with Father O'Malley. After a few more words, and a cup each of the hot coffee which Dona Santa had made, the worried group broke up for the night.

▼

Early the next morning, Father O'Malley arrived at Dindinho's house, but Mariquinha was still asleep. He told Dindinho and the *curandeiro* to let her sleep until she woke up of her own accord. In the meantime, he would be at the chapel and, if he was needed before he finished hearing confessions, to send for him immediately.

As was his usual habit, the prefect was the first in line for confession. He was followed by most of the townsfolk. After several hours of listening to sometimes petty, sometimes serious sins, and giving counsel when he felt it would help, the priest was down to the last in line. It was Zulmira.

▼

Father O'Malley bade her wait before she left the chapel. He would walk with her to her home.

Before they left, he asked, "Does anyone besides you and Mariquinha know about this?"

"No, Father."

"Will she tell anyone?"

"No. I know that she won't." Bursting into tears, she exclaimed, "I'm such a monster. How could I have done this to her? Everyone should know what I've done."

"What you've said in confession is a sacred trust. I can tell no one. I don't know whether or not to advise you to tell anyone. If anyone learns of this besides we three, it would be . . . it would be disastrous."

"But what can I do, Father?"

"I'm not sure. I'll need to think this over. But I do want you to come to Cruzeiro and see me. I'll be free to see you no matter what time of day or night it is. And I do want you to see the doctor about your headaches."

"I'll do anything you say, Father."

"Then, let's go see Mariquinha."

▼

The house was empty except for Father O'Malley and Mariquinha. Mariquinha was sitting in her hammock and Father O'Malley sat across from her, on her new bed. The open windows and doors of the house invited the cool winds to enter, making Mariquinha's room a thankful refuge from the afternoon heat. Sounds from outside were audible but muted. As if from far away came the varied sounds common to all jungle settlements; people called to one another, children screamed and laughed, farmyard animals mooed, cackled, grunted, brayed, and barked. Dona Pipira's parrot sang a drunken, unintelligible song.

It was one of those inexplicable, magic moments that occasionally come to two people, even though strangers, or disparate in age, sex, or culture. Both the middle-aged priest and the ten-year-old girl sat listening to those busy sounds from a world away, and each knew that the other was listening, yet not a word had been uttered.

When a troop of monkeys began to scream from the jungle on the other side of the Juruá, their noise, though barely distinguishable, was heard by both of the occupants of the small, airy room. It was Father O'Malley who first spoke. "Those sound like spider monkeys. Can you tell the difference?"

"They sound more like squirrel monkeys. *Papai* would know."

Those few words brought Mariquinha and Father O'Malley closer together. This was important in the situation that now existed. Mariquinha had begun to plead complete loss of memory as to what had transpired. But she was not a practiced liar. In fact, she had never told a lie until now. It was obvious to all those who knew her best that she had become evasive.

There were seven figures of authority in Guajará who would always be receptive to her. They would be there whenever she had a problem, no matter how trivial or childish. They were her parents, the prefect, the *curandeiro,* the policeman, Dona Santa (who had somehow become the matriarch of the town, but who was by no means the eldest), and there was Father O'Malley. But now, her confidences might bring some unknown calamity into her young life. Some terrible, grown-up decision was upon her. Its presence was just as much felt as the clothes she wore, the hammock upon which she sat, and the vagrant breezes that ruffled stray wisps of her soft hair.

Temporarily, Father O'Malley waived the subject of

their talk. To put her at ease he reminisced about her baptism and her first communion. He answered her query about the health of the aging Father Vicente, and she answered his queries about Bom Jesus and Fatima.

The tall priest spoke with her as he would an adult. It was his custom to treat all his parishioners alike, from the littlest to the oldest. This wasn't a studied attitude. Only occasionally did he realize that he was doing this.

Abruptly, but softly, he asked, "Do you remember the words to the song you sang?"

"No, Father."

"But you do remember what happened, don't you?"

Looking into his warm, green eyes, she knew that she couldn't lie. It was impossible.

"Yes."

"I wish I could have heard your song. Everyone said that it was the most beautiful that they had ever heard."

"Truly? People said that?"

"Yes. Did you make it up yourself?"

"I think so."

"Did you do what you did because you thought that the sun was leaving you?"

"Yes," she answered nervously. "But now he's back. It was only sundown. I was kind of foolish."

"He did apologize to you, didn't he?"

She looked to the floor and hesitated. He noticed a tear sparkle as it fell and landed on her bare foot.

"Yes, Father. How did you know?"

Before he could answer, she looked into his eyes with such terror and pleading that he wanted to take her in his arms to protect her from the fate he himself must impose upon her, kind though it would be.

"What are you going to do to me?" she asked in a tense, frightened voice.

"Mariquinha. *Queridinha*. No one is going to do anything 'to' you. All of us do want to do something 'for' you. Listen. Do you like poetry?"

"Poetry?" she asked, surprised at the abrupt change in the subject. "Yes. I love poetry. Aunt Gloria recites a poem to us once a day in school."

"I know only one poem," he continued. "I don't remember who wrote it. I learned it when I was in school. Wait a moment. It's from another language, so I'll have to translate it in my mind before I can say it."

After a pause during which he stared blankly at the wall and furrowed his brow, he recited his poem.

> Behold the wonders of the mighty deep,
> Where crabs and lobsters learn to creep,
> And little fishes learn to swim,
> And clumsy sailors tumble in.

"It's kind of a silly little poem," he said.

"Oh, no. I thought it was wonderful," she said, fascinated.

"Mariquinha, we're so much like those clumsy sailors. All of us. Sometimes we fall in. Not in the sea of course, but into troubles. And when we do, it's always nice to have someone to reach out a hand to help."

Worried that he might have been talking over her head, he asked "Do you understand what I mean?"

"Yes, Father. You want to help me."

"I do," he answered, smiling. "I do very much. Your *mamãe* and *papai* wanted me to help you. They want me to decide what's to be done. What's to become of you. And I do want to do something. But you can have a say. You can help me decide.

"First of all, I'd like for you to come to Cruzeiro with me. Do you know any of the sisters at the convent school?"

"Yes. I know Sister Theresa."

"Do you like her?"

"Yes, Father. She's very nice."

"That's perfect. She's the one I want you to talk to. I think that she will want you to stay with her and go to her school. Of course you can come home for vacations, and your parents can always visit you. Will you do this? Talk to her, I mean. You can decide about school later."

• • • • •

"Yes, I will."

"Well, then. Would your mother mind if I made us some coffee?"

"No, no. She wouldn't mind. But I know how. Let me do it."

Father O'Malley reached out and took her small hand in his and helped her from her hammock.

"Mariquinha?"

"Yes, Father?"

"Can I give you a hug?"

"Oh, yes," she said. The tears she had been holding back flowed freely, now that she was in his arms.

▼

Early the next Monday morning, just before dawn, four people walked down to the river to a waiting boat. One was Father O'Malley, who carried his suitcase. One was Dindinho, who also carried a suitcase, Mariquinha's. The third was Zulmira, and walking beside her, holding her hand, was her daughter.

As they settled into the small boat, the sun rose, bringing to all its warmth. Giving to all their very lives. The three adults glanced its way, admiring its fiery beauty, then, turned away self-consciously. Mariquinha wouldn't look even though it called to her with its fairest smile.

Epilogue

Mariquinha could hardly have guessed what her fate would be that morning when she left Guajará to stay with the sisters in Cruzeiro do Sul. The wealth that was to become hers many years later was unimaginable to anyone who came from southern Amazonas. Happiness had fled from her life, returning but once to glow briefly with the birth of her daughter in a faraway place called the Alfama. As had her father before her, she had become most expert at hiding the periods of depression that were forever to plague her.

When Sister Theresa felt that Mariquinha was well enough, she enrolled her in the school. Although she was always to have doubts about how well Mariquinha had recovered, she saw that she had not lost reality completely, and as the years passed, the nun saw that, no matter how much inner turmoil her charge was hiding, she was able to adjust to life and to cope with it as well as anyone could.

Instead of staying at the convent for one year, as had been planned, Sister Theresa implored Dindinho and Zulmira to let their daughter finish her schooling there. The little girl had become the best pupil that they had ever had. Academic life had become so easy for Mariquinha that she surpassed by far all the other students.

When Mariquinha's parents agreed to let her stay, the sisters began to prepare special courses for her. Although they were careful not to overwork her, they were constantly finding new things for her to learn. They taught her their own language, German. When she had become proficient in this tongue, they taught her English, then French. By the time she left the convent at eighteen, she had mastered typing, accounting, and most of the higher forms of math. Even old Father Vicente had lent a hand. He taught her biology, and found her the equal of any of his former students at the university where he had taught in São Paulo.

The subject which was to become more important than any of the others in her later life, and which was her favorite, was music. She learned to play the piano and the guitar, and most especially, learned to sing. Her lovely voice needed little training. She learned the songs of the church first, then studied Brazilian and Portuguese folk songs. Many times the sisters and the other students were to sit entranced as she sang for them. Some wept.

After she had left school, and had spent a year at home, she returned one day to the convent doors and asked Sister Theresa to recommend her to someone in Rio de Janeiro or São Paulo. Although she had had no further problems at home, and had become close to her mother again, she had learned of the outside world and wanted to see for herself all the wonderful places about which she had read. Mostly, however, happiness had eluded her. Perhaps she could find it elsewhere.

Sister Theresa was amenable to this. In fact, she was overjoyed. Mariquinha had too much talent and too many acquired skills to remain locked away forever in the midst of the jungle. After a long talk with Zulmira and Dindinho, who reluctantly agreed that Mariquinha was unhappy, she wrote two letters. One was to her friends in Rio de Janeiro in a convent there. She asked them, as a special favor, to allow Mariquinha to live with them until she could find good lodgings. The other letter was to a German-Brazilian import-export firm, recommending Mariquinha as an excellent typist and linguist.

Three months later, Mariquinha arrived in Rio de Janeiro and began her new life.

From this point on, little is known of Mariquinha's life. Although she often wrote to her parents, who had Fatima read her letters and write a reply, and to Sister Theresa, her words were only of new places she had seen, trivialities and reminiscences, rarely of the really important things, except for once. This was to announce her wedding to a fellow employee of the import-export company.

Her letters came less and less often, but never stopped. One such letter told them of a new job which both she and her husband had found in São Paulo. Her father, a widower now that Zulmira had died, leaving him with three children who had never known their lovely sister, had become worried that there was something that Mariquinha wasn't telling him. Occasionally she had sent to him large sums of money, and wouldn't explain from where it came. Accordingly, he asked Fatima to write to Adão, the former temporary prefect of

• • • • •
213

Guajará, who was a resident of São Paulo, to check on her.

With praise, Adão wrote back that he would speak to her, but that it really wasn't necessary. He already knew all about her. She had become one of the most popular folk singers that Brazilian café society had ever known. She was in demand everywhere. He wrote that, even though she was reclusive and avoided publicity, feasts, and fêtes, and refused recording contracts, she had become quite wealthy from her new vocation.

Dindinho hurriedly sent a telegram to Adão asking him to desist, and explained more fully in a following letter that, now that he knew what his daughter was doing, he would wait for her to tell him. But Dindinho knew that Mariquinha would never write to him and explain that she had become a singer. She knew that the only nightclubs her father had ever heard about were those that were not equated with decency. Dindinho was a wise man. He accepted the praise with which Adão had spoken of Mariquinha, and, in his heart, he became proud of her.

Four years after moving to São Paulo, Mariquinha and her husband went to Portugal, where they were to stay for the rest of their lives. For a brief two years, Mariquinha sang in the cafés of Lisbon, where she was to replace those favorites of the Portuguese, the *fadistas,* who sang their melancholy *fados* for their millions of fans. There she was adored, and was besieged from all sides with requests for appearances, with gifts, with love. After her daughter was born, she left the cafés and was never heard to sing again.

Little more was heard by the people of Guajará about their daughter of the sun. Occasionally she sent photographs of his granddaughter to Dindinho, and occasionally she wrote to others. But, as usual, her letters were only of pleasantries, with nothing of import.

Somehow, much later, a story began its rounds of the jungle town. It was said that Mariquinha was giving a free outdoor concert to the refugees of the wars in Angola, or some other exotic place, when, just at sundown, she stopped in the middle of a folk song, paused, then sang once again her beautiful paean to the sun. It was said that the stunned audience, upon recovering their senses, applauded wildly, and rushed the stage from which Mariquinha had fled in tears. And that this was the real reason that she had quit singing.

This might have happened, but it may be only a wishful tale. It's probably not true.

The Last We Hear of Bom Jesus

Maria Fatima hated change, as did the rubber tappers. Some in Guajará thought it wonderful. Most were afraid. Maybe it was good, but probably not. In any case, she hated to walk towards the south. The southern horizon was always filled with a haze of white smoke, and the smell of burning, and it seemed to get closer and hazier every day. She thought at first that the smoke was made by the workers who were building the new road from Cruzeiro, but her father explained that it was only new settlers from the *Nordeste,* clearing land for farms and ranches. That made it not so scary. Soon, people said, many would come here to live. Two families of settlers had already moved into Guajará, and they were nice people. They had children her age. But she missed Mariquinha, who was always away at school. She wished that she could go to the convent school in Cruzeiro, or that Mariquinha would come home to stay.

On this day, Fatima had to walk down the path to the south, because, according to Dindinho, that was the direction he had seen Bom Jesus taking just after dawn.

At a cross-path, she encountered *seu* Bezerra, carrying an enormous load of sugar cane on his back. He was thankful to have met Fatima. It was a relief to dump the heavy load on the ground and rest for a moment.

"*Seu* Bezerra?" she asked. "Have you seen Bom Jesus?"

"No, *moçinha*, I haven't. Wait. Yes, I did. He was running towards Dona Santa's house."

Seu Bezerra lopped off a piece of sugar cane with his machete and handed it to her. "This one is particularly juicy," he said.

She took it from him, smiled, and said, "*Obrigada,*" then left him to his burden.

It was a wonderful morning. The wildflowers waved

· · · · ·

218

at her as she passed by, and the animals and people greeted her. They did not think about the smoke to the south. She would not, either. And the sugar cane was juicy and sweet.

Fatima could see Dona Santa through her window. She was washing dishes.

"Dona Santa? Have you seen Bom Jesus?"

"Yes, I have, *menina*. He's in here taking a nap. Come in and finish off the *farofa*. Everybody left in a hurry this morning."

Fatima entered the house and sat down at the table. Dona Santa placed a plateful of warm, mealy *farofa*, fried with bits of pork, in front of her, and Bom Jesus ran up and jumped into her lap.

Between mouthfuls, Fatima asked, "Dona Santa, do you think that the *curandeiro* will get better?"

"No, *menina*. I don't think so. He's very ill, and very old."

"I think Bom Jesus and I are going to visit him," Fatima said.

"Are you? that's what I was going to do. I was going to take a pot of fish soup to him. Can you take it for me? It's not heavy."

"I'd love to. I wanted to take him something, but I didn't know what he needed."

As she and Bom Jesus left Dona Santa's house, she

• • • • •
219

asked and received her blessing. She was headed north now. The sky ahead was blue and cloudless, filled with singing birds.

She was stopped once more–this time by Moacyr Velho, who called to her from the doorway of his *botequim,* and asked her and Bom Jesus to taste some of the new batch of ginger-beer he had brewed. They stayed awhile, but then Bom Jesus ran down the path a ways, and stopped and stared back at her, telling her it was time to go.

▼

As Fatima entered the *curandeiro*'s old house, she noticed that someone, probably Zé Maia, had replaced the rickety steps with hard, new lumber. The roof had many holes in it, and was bulging inward, but she knew that later that day Dindinho and Edison Graça were going to build a new one. The *curandeiro* had taken care of the villagers when they were in need–now it was their turn to care for him.

The early morning sunlight came into the house from the doors and the windows, and from the many-holed roof. The room was aglow and warm. But under the bed upon which the *curandeiro* lay, in the shadows, was a darkness abiding. Fatima saw this, and looked away. She looked into the *curandeiro*'s eyes and saw the same darkness, then stared at his bristly chin as he spoke.

"Fatima," he said. "How wonderful. I was just now thinking about you."

"I brought some fish soup that Dona Santa made, and a bottle of ginger-beer from Moacyr Velho."

"Come sit on the bed and stay awhile," he said.

As Fatima went to the bed, Bom Jesus ran up and joined them. "My favorite cat," the old man said, as he weakly rubbed his fur.

Fatima laughed. "He *has* to be your favorite cat, because he's the only one in Guajará."

The *curandeiro* smiled. "You're right. Cats don't last long around here. But he's still my favorite."

"*Seu* Estevão?" Fatima asked. "May I do anything for you?"

"No, *menina*. Just visiting me is enough. Fatima? Why won't you look at me?"

She turned and looked into his eyes once more, but quickly averted her face.

"*Queridinha*. Don't cry. I understand. I know what you see. I'm very old, and you are very young, but we're very much alike. We know when someone is happy, and we can see when people are hurt inside. We know when a woman is going to have a baby, even before she does, and we know when old ones are . . ." He paused, then said, "Oh, Fatima. You would have been a fine *curandeira*."

"Do you think so, *seu* Estevão? Please teach me. I already know the names of all the trees and plants, but I don't know how to make medicines from them. You can tell me how. When you're . . . when you're gone, there'll be no one."

"Of all the people in the village," he said, with sadness in his voice, "there have been only two who would make good *curandeiros*. *Seu* Adão: but he didn't want to be one, and then, there's you. But you're so young, and you don't know how unhappy you would be."

He placed his thin, callused hand on her forehead. "Guajará will have a doctor soon," he said.

"I know," she answered.

"You could become his assistant?"

"I will be his assistant, but I can be a *curandeira*, too."

"I suppose," he said. "It couldn't hurt to teach you about herbs, and how to make small remedies. You go home and ask your mother and father. If they refuse, I can't go against their wishes. If they accept, then I want you to think—think very hard about the consequences. You'll be called upon day and night, and you'll see people—your friends—very sick and dying, and you'll feel guilty because you can't help them. You'll be unhappy. Think very hard. Then, if you still want to learn, come back in two weeks."

• • • • •

"Two weeks!"

"Look at me, Fatima." She looked, and though his face was gaunt and pale, the darkness in his eyes was gone. "I'll be here," he smiled.

"You will," she answered with wonder.

▼

Afterwards, Fatima stood outside the *curandeiro*'s house, thinking on what he had said. Bom Jesus waited with her awhile, then began walking along the path into the jungle. Of course Fatima followed. For her, Bom Jesus was not only a friend, but also a guardian. Fatima, now still a child, almost a woman, loved to wander in the high jungles. Something unthinkable. Something to hide from her *mamãe* and *papai* with all the secretiveness her young wiles could contrive. Times uncountable she had been warned of giant boa constrictors, bushmasters, and preying jaguars. Only men could love such a place.

But with Bom Jesus at her side, she felt as safe as if she were asleep in her own bed. He taught her all the hidden pathways and game trails. Fatima learned as well as any woodsman how to find her way home. She learned that you shouldn't worry about poisonous snakes in this verdant parkland. They were seldom seen. Boa constrictors were to be petted if they were small, walked around if they were large. Pumas, jaguars, and other dangerous beasts, well, with Bom Jesus at her side, they wouldn't dare.

And they didn't dare. On some mysterious occasions, Bom Jesus would rush, growling, piebald fur on end, at some rustling underbrush, quickly chasing away some never-seen enemy. But these were rare occasions indeed. Mostly they just walked for endless hours, marveling at the green loveliness enclosing them.

You say that it seems a green hell to you? Yes, if you waded forbidding swamps or fought your way through low thickets. A green hell, the high jungle? No. Not if you were akin to Fatima and Bom Jesus. Oh, those wonderful times spent walking, sometimes running through that lost world of green, of ever-present, omnipotent green. There were pretty wonders to sit and watch. An occasional bright sunbeam, alive with happily waltzing jungle dust, would find its way through the tree-shadows. Iridescent butterflies and small birds wafted throughout, as if to laugh in the face of the death that awaited in those shadows. In the high jungle, the undergrowth was starved for sunlight, hating the greedy trees that kept it away. Stunted it was. As easily traversed as if it were close-cropped pasture land.

How many times, oh times without end, had Fatima and Bom Jesus rested on fallen, mossy logs, counting the giant, blue, harmless mosquitoes who floated with each soft breeze, becoming round puffballs, wills-o'-the-wisp? How many families of ring-tailed, pointy-snouted coatis did they silently snoop upon as they rooted and romped their way down hidden trails? And those noisy, nosy monkeys high overhead—tiny black ones, manlike balls of fur; spider monkeys, skinny, long-limbed dance masters of the treetops; and, sometimes, a troop of howler monkeys who made deliciously scary noises as big as the world. Oh, yes, and the parrots—raucous, messy beings.

Away from the *piuns,* from the hot, dusty, muddy, flea-, fly-, gnat-, and mosquito-ridden banks of the river—softly blown by invisible wood nymphs—the almost unfelt wind cooled magically, beckoning.

But most of all, there was the misty emerald in which Fatima and Bom Jesus' world was enclosed. Green. Greener than Father O'Malley's eyes. Greener than . . . but there is no such word. Just eternally green. A rainbow's hue that sang bewitching songs.

Oh, times without end.

Yet end they must. End as all things so sadly do.

▼

Do mornings know things? Are they sentient? This particular morning must have been. The hallowed old trees smiled at Fatima and Bom Jesus. The iridescent butterflies danced their liveliest. The sunbeams shone their brightest.

There was one difference. The silence. No noisy parrots or monkeys or coatis. No tiny, nervous deer. No mice. No noise. Quietude, foreboding. Echoes of falling leaves.

For the green forest's sad friend, death, stalked its byways.

There, in front of the two companions, it stood. There in all its handsome, hungry majesty, was a much-feared entity. Jaguar was his name. Spotted, of sleek coat, muscled with awesome strength, ravenous of belly.

Fatima was very frightened, and only barely remembers what happened next. When the jaguar's muscles tensed for one deadly leap, Bom Jesus's hair stood on end. He became maddened by the fate awaiting his raven-haired Fatima. He charged the jaguar.

The great predator, not usually a coward, knew that with one bite he could crush forever this absurd bit of charging, yowling fur. Yet, somehow, he knew also that the cost might be dear. Or, perhaps, he feared the madness he saw in the squinting blue eyes. He turned and ran the other way.

Bom Jesus and the jaguar vanished forever. If one is prone to rationalize such things, maybe Bom Jesus lost